Words Their Way™

Letter Name–Alphabetic Sorts for Spanish-Speaking English Learners

Lori Helman
University of Minnesota

Donald R. Bear
University of Nevada, Reno

Marcia Invernizzi
University of Virginia

Shane Templeton
University of Nevada, Reno

Francine Johnston
University of North Carolina, Greensboro

Allyn & Bacon
is an imprint of

PEARSON

Boston   New York   San Francisco
Mexico City   Montreal   Toronto   London   Madrid   Munich   Paris
Hong Kong   Singapore   Tokyo   Cape Town   Sydney

Vice President and Executive Publisher: Jeffery W. Johnston
Senior Editor: Linda Ashe Bishop
Senior Development Editor: Hope Madden
Senior Project Manager: Mary M. Irvin
Editorial Assistant: Demetrius Hall
Senior Art Director: Diane C. Lorenzo
Additional Illustrations: Jeremy Sengly
Cover Designer: Ali Mohrman
Cover Image: Hope Madden
Operations Specialist: Matthew Ottenweller
Director of Marketing: Quinn Perkson
Marketing Manager: Krista Clark
Marketing Coordinator: Brian Mounts

For related title and support materials, visit our online catalog at www.pearsonhighered.com

Library of Congress Cataloging-in-Publication Data

Words their way: letter name-alphabetic sorts for Spanish-speaking English learners / by Lori Helman . . . [et al.].
   p. cm.
  Includes bibliographical references.
  ISBN-13: 978-0-13-242103-4
  ISBN-10: 0-13-242103-8
  1. English language—Study and teaching—Spanish speakers. 2. Word recognition. 3. English language—Orthography and spelling. I. Helman, Lori.
  PE1129.S8W67 2009
  420'.4261—dc22

2008008993

10 9 8 7 6 5 4 3 2 1   [BRR]   12 11 10 09 08

Allyn & Bacon
is an imprint of

Contents

Preface

Words Their Way: Letter Name-Alphabetic Sorts for Spanish-Speaking English Learners is designed to supplement the text *Words Their Way with English Learners: Word Study for Phonics, Vocabulary, and Spelling Instruction.* That core text provides a practical, research-based and classroom-proven way to study words with students. This supplemental text provides a complete word study curriculum for letter name-alphabetic spellers from Spanish-speaking backgrounds by focusing on the similarities and differences between English and Spanish and how to use that information to support students as they learn English. The materials provided in this text will also complement the use of any existing phonics, spelling, and reading curricula.

The curriculum outlined in this text is designed to scaffold students by 1) building on students' vocabularies in Spanish and the sounds that are common to both English and Spanish letters; 2) starting with the most common and high-utility English words; 3) teaching vocabulary through pictures and word-picture matching; and 4) providing opportunities to explicitly compare and work with sounds in English that may require extra help for Spanish speakers.

Words Their Way: Letter Name-Alphabetic Sorts for Spanish-Speaking English Learners provides teachers with prepared reproducible sorts and step-by-step directions on how to guide students through the sorting lesson. There are organizational tips as well as follow-up activities to extend the lesson through weekly routines.

Who are letter name-alphabetic spellers? Learners in this stage have progressed beyond making random marks and representational drawings in their writing, and they use initial and final consonants with some consistency in both reading and writing. English learners in the early part of this stage often need extra help mastering specific initial and final consonants that are distinct from sounds in Spanish. Once this foundation is set, students will be ready to begin the study of blends and digraphs through picture sorts, words families, and short vowels in CVC patterns.

In terms of reading development, letter name-alphabetic spellers are typically beginning readers. Spanish speakers in this stage of reading in English vary in the levels of literacy and oral abilities in English. Students will also vary widely in their home language literacy skills. It is common to find students of all ages in the letter name-alphabetic stage of spelling. Elementary and secondary students in this stage find these activities meaningful.

How to use the materials and where to begin. The assessments provided in the core text (*Words Their Way with English Learners*) show where your students range on the developmental continuum. Begin word study based on an assessment of the features students know, and the ones they are trying out, something we observe in the spelling inventories presented in Chapter 2 of *Words their Way with English Learners (WTW EL)*. The assessments guide you to the features and the stage. When it is clear that a student is in the letter name-alphabetic stage, then discern where *within* this stage the student's spelling is developmentally. In the table of contents, find exactly where to begin in the sorts based on the student's errors. You will see specialized sorts that you may want to choose. Remember to begin where the sorts are relatively familiar and work into the more difficult sorts and contrasts.

Overview

Words Their Way: Letter Name–Alphabetic Sorts for Spanish-Speaking English Learners is a companion volume to Words Their Way with English Learners: Word Study for Phonics, Vocabulary, and Spelling Instruction (WTW EL). It is a good idea to have this core text on hand for its assessments, additional sorts, and presentations of developmental word knowledge and research base. Refer specifically to Chapter 5 in WTW EL for its collection of activities and picture and word sorts for students in the letter name–alphabetic stage of spelling.

For the sorts in this supplement, students should have a good grasp of many consonant sounds. English learners at this level are found throughout the elementary grades depending on their school experiences. To determine exactly where individual students and small groups should start within this supplement, administer one of the spelling inventories and use the feature guides from Chapter 2 and the Appendix in WTW EL.

SCOPE AND SEQUENCE OF THIS BOOK

This book begins with a series of five concept sorts (Unit I) that help students learn sorting procedures, teach essential vocabulary in English, and serve as preassessments of students' oral English skills. Next, Unit II reviews beginning consonant sounds that are similar in English and Spanish; for students who are just beginning to learn English, the sorts may also be conducted in Spanish. Unit III reviews consonant sounds that are different in Spanish and English. Unit IV focuses on specific consonant sounds that may be most difficult for Spanish speakers. To conclude the work on initial sounds, Unit V focuses on digraphs and blends, and then contrasts sounds that may be confusing for Spanish speakers.

Unit VI features ending sounds, which often differ between words in Spanish and English. Following this, Unit VII turns to vowel sounds, first helping students to identify the sounds of the short vowels, and then moving into picture and word sorts with short-vowel word families. Unit IX is the first introduced with only words. At this point, students have had many experiences with the key words and sounds, and should be comfortable with the English vocabulary.

Unit X through Unit XIII contrast difficult sounds in words such as ending sounds with close contrasts (e.g., /d/ and /t/), short-vowel sounds (e.g., short *e* and short *i*), beginning digraphs or blends (e.g., /ch/ and /sh/), and ending digraphs or blends (e.g., /ng/ and /nt/). The more difficult these contrasts are for students to perceive, the more you will want to work at an in-depth pace on these sorts.

RESOURCES

Each unit's *Notes for the Teacher* provides placement guidelines and background information about the features of study. This section also describes weekly routines that ensure practice and enrichment and offers suggestions for *Literature Connections* and games. Directions for how to introduce the sort, along with additional teaching tips, are provided for each lesson. Sorts are presented as black line masters that can be reproduced so that students can sort their words a number of times. We recommend that you enlarge the sorts about 10% to maximize the print size. You should also use the masters to prepare a set of pictures and words for modeling. You may want to make a transparency of the sort and cut it apart for use on an overhead or enlarge the words on the copier or write them for use in a pocket chart. You can also simply make your own copy to cut apart and use on a desktop or on the floor. See *WTW EL* for additional background information, organizational tips, games, and activities. The core text *Words Their Way: Word Study for Phonics, Vocabulary, and Spelling Instruction* (Fourth Edition) *(WTW)* provides additional resources, including a CD-ROM with reproducible sorts, and a DVD with classroom vignettes for you and students to watch.

PLACEMENT AND PACING

This book contains 13 units of study that flow in difficulty from early to middle to late features in the letter name–alphabetic stage. Following are general guidelines for placing students using the results of their qualitative spelling inventories.

Early letter name–alphabetic spellers know most of their letter sound correspondences for consonants but may still confuse *y* and *w*, *b* and *p*, or sounds that are difficult for Spanish speakers to distinguish in English such as *d* and *t*. Vowels are used sparingly. Students earn some points (5–6) on the Primary Spelling Inventory in the initial and final consonants columns, but do not spell any words correctly. They benefit from a review of initial consonants and then move into the sorts that contrast difficult beginning and ending sounds using picture support. If students are missing three or more initial consonants they need to spend extended time with the beginning consonant sorts in this book, or work further on consonants as described in Chapter 4 of *WTW EL*.

English learners in the letter name–alphabetic stage may be able to perceive the correct number of sounds that a word contains, but have difficulty distinguishing the correct sound because of a confusion with a sound in Spanish. Units IV through VII are primarily designed to help students work with these contrasts, and to help you identify areas in which students need extra support. Let these sorts be assessments to guide your instruction with students; spend time on the sorts and contrasts you see your students needing.

Middle letter name–alphabetic spellers know initial and final consonants (earning 6 or 7 points in both categories on the Primary Spelling Inventory) and they also use but confuse some medial short vowels (scoring 0 to 2 points for short vowels). They earn few if any points for blends and digraphs. They now study blends and digraphs in word sorts with some picture support, such as the word family sorts in Unit VIII.

Late letter name–alphabetic spellers spell some short vowels correctly (earning 2 to 4 points in that category) as well as many blends and digraphs (earning 4 to 7 points on those features). Sorts 73 to 77 focus on short-vowel words with blends and digraphs. If students are spelling most short vowels (earning 5 to 6 points) correctly AND most blends and digraphs (5 to 7 points) AND are using but confusing long-vowel markers, then they are ready to begin the study of long vowels. Sorts for students in this next stage are found in *Word Sorts for Within Word Pattern Spellers*.

The 13 spell checks can be used as pretests to gather in-depth information about features and to place your students more accurately. For example, you might give Spell Check 8 (page 120) to assess students' knowledge of word families. If students spell 90% on a spell check correctly, then you can safely move on to the next feature.

As you can see, not every student needs every sort in this text. The book is designed to provide you with a comprehensive set of sorts to use with the standard features all letter name–alphabetic students learn, as well as the difficult oral contrasts that Spanish-speaking students may experience. The pacing for these sorts is designed for slow growth, with great depth. After finding that your students need to work on a specific feature and identifying the appropriate sort, spend 3 to 5 days following routines that encourage students to practice for mastery. If your students seem to be catching on quickly, you can speed up the pace by spending fewer days on a sort or you may skip some sorts altogether. If you find, however, that students are not understanding the features or contrasts that are presented, you need to slow the pace and perhaps even create additional sorts for some students using pictures and word lists throughout this book and in the main text. *WTW EL* has 217 sorts outlined in the Appendix that provide in-depth contrasts for English Learners (ELLs) in the letter name–alphabetic stage. Templates to create these additional sorts can be found in this book's Appendix.

Unit 1   Concept Sorts for Vocabulary Development

NOTES FOR THE TEACHER

A concept sort is an activity in which pictures, objects, or words are grouped by shared attributes. These five picture sorts are designed to build vocabulary and critical thinking skills and teach the process of sorting. These sorts are especially useful at the beginning of the school year so that you can informally assess your students' oral language skills in English. Watch to see if students understand your directions for doing a closed sort in which you name the categories, and then categorize the pictures appropriately. Note how they sort the items when they have an opportunity to do a sort of their own categorizing. Are students able to describe their work in Spanish, or in English using single words or phrases, or in complete sentences? Which words do students know, and which will they need instruction to learn? Use these sorts to support your vocabulary instruction and to create other language-rich activities to get your students talking.

Standard Weekly Routines for Use with Sorts 1–5

1. *Learn and Practice Unknown Vocabulary.*   Preview the pictures from the sort with your students. Name each picture, and have students repeat the name. Next, ask students to name the pictures. Set aside words that are unknown so they can be practiced. Select up to 10 of the unknown pictures for vocabulary study. Talk about the pictures with students, clarify their meanings, and invite students to use them in simple sentences. If possible, have students share the names of the pictures in Spanish.

2. *Repeated Work with the Pictures.*   Students should repeat the sort several times after it has been modeled and discussed under your directions. Make a copy of the black line master for each student, enlarging it to reduce paper waste and increase the size. Provide opportunities for them to create their own categories for the sort, and to share their ideas with others. After cutting out the pictures and using them for individual practice, the pieces can be stored in an envelope or plastic bag to sort again several times on other days. See *WTW EL* for tips on managing picture sorting.

3. *Picture Hunts and Picture Dictionaries.*   Students can look through magazines, catalogs, and newspaper ads for pictures of things to add to their concept sorts. Encourage students to share their findings and create personal picture dictionaries so they can reference the vocabulary in the future.

4. *Games and Other Activities.*   Many games such as Concentration, I Spy, Charades, and Bingo are outlined in *WTW EL*. These will help you use the concept sort cards for vocabulary and language development activities.

Sort 1 Around Town

Items in the Around Town Concept Sort		
(store)	(parking lot)	(office building)
(post office)	(park)	(school)
(street)	(sidewalk)	(parking meter)
(mailbox)	(restaurant)	(flag)
(stoplight)	(bus stop)	(gas station)
(neighborhood)	(zoo)	(movie theater)

Demonstrate, Sort, Check, and Reflect

(See page 13.)

1. Prepare a set of pictures for teacher-directed modeling. Practice the vocabulary with students as described in the standard weekly routines on page 5.

2. Begin a concept sort by stating your thinking aloud as you model for your students: *There are lots of pictures here of things I see around town. Some of these pictures are of places I can go into, others are not places. Let's make two groups—places I can go into, and things that are not places.* Hold up the picture of a school. *This is a picture of a _____? School, yes. A school is a place I go into in town. I am going to put the school at the top so we can put other pictures of places underneath. What about a store? Is a store a place I can go into? Yes, I will put the store underneath the picture of the school.* Now pick up something that is not a place, such as a parking meter. *This is a picture of a parking meter. Is a parking meter a place I can go into? No! Let's make a different column for things that are not places I can go into.* Continue working your way through each item to decide where it will go—underneath either the school picture or the parking meter picture. Encourage students to participate in your decision making as you go. If there is an item that does not fit easily into either column, then you can decide if it should be shared between the two or if it belongs in an oddball column.

3. Next demonstrate how to check, correct, and reflect: *When we are all done, we read our columns and check our work. If we find one that does not belong, we make a change.* Read the pictures in each column, adjusting if necessary. Restate why you sorted the way you did.

Beginning of Around Town Concept Sort

4. Give students their own set of Around Town picture cards for use in sorting. Allow them to repeat your sort, or think of a new way to sort the items. Have students tell you and others in their group how they sorted their pictures. Have them read the items in their groups, and check them. Listen to the language your students are using, and take advantage of opportunities to repeat the names of unknown words.

Extend

On subsequent days, see if students can think of even more ways to sort their picture cards. Have them play guessing games with a partner to identify the names of the pictures. Put the picture cards in plastic bags and have students take them home to practice with their families. Look in print materials around the classroom for examples of places and things around town to discuss. Glue the pictures into individual dictionaries for students to refer to as they learn new words in English. Read and discuss some of the pictures and stories from the *Literature Connection* below.

Literature Connection

Ancona, G. (1998). *Barrio: El barrio de José/Barrio: Jose's neighborhood*. New York: Harcourt. Spanish edition available from Lectorum Publishers.

Bogan, P. (2002). *Spike in the city*. New York: Putnam Juvenile.

Bourgeois, P. (2002). *Franklin va al hospital/Franklin goes to the hospital*. New York: Scholastic. Spanish edition available from Lectorum Publishers.

Brown, M. (2003). *D.W. y el carné de biblioteca/D.W.'s library card*. New York: Little Brown Young Readers. Spanish edition available from Lectorum Publishers.

Emberley, R. (1990). *Talking a walk: A book in two languages*. New York: Little, Brown.

Johnson, S. T. (1999). *Alphabet city*. New York: Puffin.

Johnson, S. T. (2003). *City by numbers*. New York: Puffin.

Llewellyn, C. (2006). *Watch out! Around town*. Hauppauge, NY: Barron's Educational Series.

Neubecker, R. (2004). *Wow! City!* New York: Hyperion.

Olson, N. (2007). *Ovals around town* (and others in the A+ series). Mankato, MN: Capstone Press.

Sis, P. (2000). *Madlenka*. New York: Farrar, Strauss & Giroux.

Sort 2 Animals

Items in the Animals Concept Sort		
(cat)	(dog)	(fish)
(pig)	(snail)	(bird)
(cow)	(duck)	(fox)
(spider)	(whale)	(horse)
(rat)	(monkey)	(bear)
(lion)	(skunk)	(squirrel)

Demonstrate, Sort, Check, and Reflect

(See page 14.)

1. Prepare a set of pictures for teacher-directed modeling. Practice the vocabulary with students as described in the standard weekly routines on page 5.

2. Begin the concept sort by stating your thinking aloud as you model for your students: *This sort has lots of pictures of animals. Let's try sorting the animals in different ways.* Hold up the picture of a cow. *This is a picture of a _____? Cow, yes. A cow is an animal that we might find on a farm. I am going to put the cow at the top so we can put other pictures of animals that live on the farm underneath. What about a monkey? Does a monkey live on a farm? No, I will put the monkey at the top also so we can put animals that do not live on a farm underneath.* Now pick up another animal card, such as a pig. *This is a picture of a pig. Is a pig a farm animal? Yes! Let's put the pig below the cow because it is also a farm animal.* Continue working your way through each animal to decide where it will go—underneath either the cow picture or the monkey picture. Encourage students to participate in your decision making as you go. If there is an animal that does not fit easily into either column, then you can decide if it should be shared between the two or if it belongs in an oddball column.

3. Next demonstrate how to check, correct, and reflect: *When we are all done, we read our columns and check our work. If we find one that does not belong, we make a change.* Read the pictures in each column, adjusting if necessary. Restate why you sorted the way you did.

4. Give students their own set of animal picture cards for use in sorting. Allow them to repeat your sort, or think of a new way to sort the items. Have students tell you and others in their group how they sorted their pictures. Have them read the items in their groups, and check them. Listen to the language your students are using, and take advantage of opportunities to repeat the names of unknown words, or build sentences with the words as students' language skills allow.

Extend

On subsequent days, see if students can think of even more ways to sort their picture cards, such as by the number of legs, whether or not it can swim, or if it has fur. Have them play guessing games with a partner to identify the names of the pictures. Put the picture cards in plastic bags and have students take them home to practice with their families. Look in print materials around the classroom for examples of animals to discuss. Have the students tell or dictate stories of animals they have come into contact with. Glue the pictures into individual dictionaries for students to refer to as they learn new words in English. Read and discuss some of the pictures and stories from the *Literature Connection* below.

Literature Connection

Guarino, D., Kellogg, S., & Marcuse, A. (1992). *Is your mama a llama?* New York: Scholastic. Spanish edition available from Lectorum Publishers.

Harter, D. (2005). *The animal boogie.* Cambridge, MA: Barefoot Books.

Miller, J. (1987). *The farm alphabet book.* New York: Scholastic.

Priddy, R. (2002). *My big animal book* (and others in the Big Ideas for Little People series). New York: St. Martin's Press.

Provensen, A., & Provensen, M. (2001). *Our animal friends at Maple Hill Farm.* New York: Aladdin.

Spier, P. (1992). *Noah's ark.* New York: Random House.

Sort 3 Clothes

Items in the Clothes Concept Sort		
(pants)	(dress)	(shirt)
(skirt)	(hat)	(belt)
(jacket)	(vest)	(wig)
(Tee-shirt)	(sweater)	(coat)
(shorts)	(socks)	(shoe)
(tie)	(suit)	(scarf)

Demonstrate, Sort, Check, and Reflect

(See page 15.)

1. Prepare a set of pictures for teacher-directed modeling. Practice the vocabulary with students as described in the standard weekly routines on page 5.
2. Begin the concept sort by stating your thinking aloud as you model for your students: *This sort has lots of pictures of things we wear—clothes. Let's try sorting the clothes in different ways.* Demonstrate the sort as has been described in Sorts 1 and 2. You might categorize the clothing by if you would wear it on a cold day or a hot day, or by whether it goes on the feet, legs, torso, or head.
3. Next check, correct, and reflect with the students: *Let's read our columns and check our work. If we find one that does not belong, we will make a change.* Read the pictures in each column, adjusting if necessary. Restate why you sorted the way you did.
4. Give students their own set of clothes picture cards for use in sorting. Allow them to repeat your sort, or think of a new way to sort the items. Have students tell you and others in their group how they sorted their pictures. Have them read the items in their groups, and check them. Listen to the language your students are using, and take advantage of opportunities to repeat the names of unknown words, or build sentences to extend students' language skills.

Extend

On subsequent days, see if students can think of even more ways to sort their picture cards. Have them play guessing games with a partner to identify the names of the pictures. Put the picture cards in plastic bags and have students take them home to practice with their families. Glue the pictures into individual dictionaries for students to refer to as they learn new words in English. Do a directed drawing with students by having them draw and color specific pieces of clothing onto their paper doll figure such as, "Draw a red T-shirt and black shoes on your picture." Read and discuss some of the pictures and stories from the *Literature Connection* below.

Literature Connection

Ahlberg, A. (2005). *The man who wore all his clothes.* London: Walker Books, Ltd.

Emberly, R. (2002). *My clothes/Mi ropa.* New York: Little Brown and Company.

London, J. (1994). *Froggy gets dressed.* New York: Puffin Books. Spanish edition available from Lectorum Publishers.

Neitzel, S. (1994). *The jacket I wear in the snow.* New York: HarperTrophy.

Peek, M. (2006). *Mary wore her red dress.* New York: Clarion Books.

Rosa-Mendoza, G. (2004). *My clothes/Mi ropa.* Wheaton, IL: Me+Mi Publishing.

Sort 4 Grocery Store

Items in the Grocery Store Concept Sort		
(milk)	(bread)	(soup)
(juice)	(fish to eat)	(meat)
(apple)	(cheese)	(ice cream)
(chicken)	(beans)	(rice)
(potatoes)	(yogurt)	(bananas)
(lettuce)	(gum)	(nut)

Demonstrate, Sort, Check, and Reflect

(See page 16.)

1. Prepare a set of pictures for teacher-directed modeling. Practice the vocabulary with students as described in the standard weekly routines on page 5.
2. Begin the concept sort by stating your thinking aloud as you model for your students: *This sort has lots of pictures of things we can buy at the grocery store. Let's try sorting the pictures in different ways.* Demonstrate the sort as described in Sorts 1 and 2. You might categorize the groceries by things that are kept in the refrigerator or not, or things that are sweet or not.
3. Next check, correct, and reflect with the students: *Let's read our columns and check our work. If we find one that does not belong, we will make a change.* Read the pictures in each column, adjusting if necessary. Restate why you sorted the way you did.
4. Give students their own set of grocery store picture cards for use in sorting. Allow them to repeat your sort, or think of a new way to sort the items. Have students tell you and others in their group how they sorted their pictures. Have them read the items in their groups, and check them. Listen to the language your students are using, and take advantage of opportunities to repeat the names of unknown words, or build sentences to extend students' language skills.

Extend

On subsequent days, see if students can think of even more ways to sort their picture cards. Have them play guessing games with a partner to identify the names of the pictures. Put the picture cards in plastic bags and have students take them home to practice with their families. Glue the pictures into individual dictionaries for students to refer to as they learn new words in English. Look through old magazines or newspaper ads for photos of grocery items to cut up and create a shopping list. Read and discuss some of the pictures and stories from the *Literature Connection* below.

Literature Connection

Brown, M. (1997). *Stone soup.* New York: Aladdin Books. Spanish edition available from Lectorum Publications.

Cousins, L. (2001). *Maisy goes shopping.* Cambridge, MA: Candlewick Press.

Ehlert, L. (1994). *Eating the alphabet.* New York: Harcourt.

Ehlert, L. (1990). *Growing vegetable soup.* New York: Harcourt. Spanish edition available from Lectorum Publishers.

Fleming, D. (1998). *Lunch.* New York: Henry Holt & Co.

Leeper, A. (2004). *Grocery store (Field trip!).* Portsmouth, NH: Heinneman. Spanish edition also available.

Mayer, M. (1998). *Just shopping with Mom.* New York: Random House Books for Young Readers.

Sort 5 Actions

Items in the Actions Concept Sort		
(sit)	(hop)	(dig)
(jog)	(nap)	(dive)
(swim)	(jump rope)	(climb)
(lift)	(dance)	(walk)
(run)	(bounce)	(play)
(kick)	(hear)	(throw)

Demonstrate, Sort, Check, and Reflect

(See page 17.)

1. Prepare a set of pictures for teacher-directed modeling. Practice the vocabulary with students as described in the standard weekly routines on page 5.
2. Begin the concept sort by stating your thinking aloud as you model for your students: *This sort shows us lots of things we can do with our bodies, like run or swim. Let's try sorting the pictures in different ways.* Demonstrate the sort as described in Sorts 1 and 2. You might categorize the pictures by actions we do slowly or we do quickly, or things we do outside versus things we do inside. If there is an action that does not fit easily into either column, then you can decide if it should be shared between the two or if it belongs in an oddball column.
3. Next, check, correct, and reflect with the students: *Let's read our columns and check our work. If we find one that does not belong, we will make a change.* Read the pictures in each column, adjusting if necessary. Restate why you sorted the way you did.
4. Give students their own set of action picture cards for use in sorting. Allow them to repeat your sort, or think of a new way to sort the items. Have students tell you and others in their group how they sorted their pictures. Have them read the items in their groups, and check them. Listen to the language your students are using, and take advantage of opportunities to repeat the names of unknown words, or build sentences to extend students' language skills.

Extend

On subsequent days, see if students can think of even more ways to sort their picture cards. Have them play guessing games with a partner to identify the names of the pictures. Put the picture cards in plastic bags and have students take them home to practice with their families. Glue the pictures into individual dictionaries for students to refer to as they learn new words in English. Play Charades with the cards to practice identifying different actions. Read and discuss some of the pictures and stories from the *Literature Connection* below.

Literature Connection

Brown, M. W. (2006). *The runaway bunny.* New York: HarperTrophy. Spanish edition available from Rayo Publishers.

Carle, E. (2007). *From head to toe.* New York: HarperFestival. Spanish edition available from Lectorum Publishers.

Kalan, R. (1989). *Jump frog jump.* New York: HarperTrophy. Spanish edition available from Greenwillow Publishers.

Raffi. (1988). *Shake my sillies out.* New York: Crown Books for Young Readers.

Shannon, D. (1999). *No, David!* New York: Scholastic. Spanish edition available from Editorial Everest.

Shannon, D. (2002). *David gets in trouble.* New York: Scholastic. Spanish edition available from Scholastic.

ASSESSMENT OF CONCEPT SORTS

Use the concept sorts to informally assess your students in two areas: vocabulary knowledge and sorting procedures. Consider the following questions.

1. *Vocabulary Knowledge.*   How many of the pictures can students identify? Are they able to say the words in English, in Spanish, both, or neither? Do they use the words in simple sentences, or have an extended conversation about the items? Notice the level of word and sentence knowledge students have so that you can build on their abilities in future word study activities.

2. *Knowledge of Sorting Procedures.*   Are students able to do the concept sorts on their own? Do they copy your sort, or come up with an independent idea? Do they follow the procedures of checking and reflecting on their sorts? What aspects of the sorting process are difficult for them and may require further instruction?

SORT 1 Around Town

SORT 2　Animals

SORT 3   Clothes

SORT 4   Grocery Store

SORT 5   Actions

Unit II   Review Sorts for Beginning Consonants: Similar Sounds in English and Spanish

NOTES FOR THE TEACHER

These picture sorts are designed to review the beginning consonants, and give you information about your students' letter sound knowledge. These first four sorts feature letters that have similar sounds in English and Spanish. Many of the items used in the sorts begin with the same sound in English and Spanish. When this is not possible, you will see a selection of the most common and useful vocabulary words in English so that students will know them for future sorts. A list of the names of pictures in English and Spanish is included in the Extend section of this chapter. For students who are just beginning to speak English, consider doing the sorts in Spanish as a way to introduce them into English phonics.

A review of beginning consonants is especially useful for first graders at the beginning of the year, and for all students in the early letter name stage. If students have missed only one or two consonants on a spelling inventory and you see that they are representing most consonants correctly in their writing, then a fast-paced review, doing a new sort every 3 to 4 days, may be all that is needed. Students who are still confusing many initial consonants probably need a slower pace, spending a week on each sort. You may want to use Spell Check 1 on page 28 as a pretest to see which children need a review of initial consonants, and which consonants need to be reviewed.

Standard Weekly Routines for Use with Sorts 6–9

1. *Learn and Practice Unknown Vocabulary.*   Preview the pictures from the sort with your students. Name each picture, and have students repeat the name. Next, ask students to name the pictures. Set aside words that are unknown so they can be practiced. Select up to 10 of the unknown pictures for vocabulary study. Talk about the pictures with students, clarify their meanings, and invite students to use them in simple sentences. If possible, have students share the names of the pictures in their home languages.

2. *Repeated Work with the Pictures.*   Students should repeat the sort several times after it has been modeled and discussed under your directions. Make a copy of the black line master for each student, enlarging it to reduce paper waste and increase the size. Provide opportunities for them to create their own categories for the sort, and to share their ideas with others. Only include the new vocabulary in independent sorts when you are sure students have learned the word. After cutting out the pictures and using them for individual practice, the pieces can be stored in an envelope or plastic bag to sort again several times on other days. See *WTW EL* for tips on managing picture sorting.

3. *Draw and Label and Cut and Paste.*   For seat work, students can draw and label pictures of things that begin with the target sounds/letters. They can also look for pictures in magazines and catalogs and paste those into categories by beginning sound. The pictures from the black line sort can be also pasted into categories and children can be asked to label the pictures. This can serve as an assessment tool but *do not* expect accurate spelling of the entire word at this time.

4. *Word or Picture Hunts and Word Banks.*   Students can look through their word banks, catalogs, and reading materials for words or pictures of things that have the targeted consonant sounds. Alphabet books are also a good place to look for additional words that begin with targeted sounds. Plan a time for students to share their findings. Words can be recorded on a group chart or students can create individual collages of cutout pictures that begin with the target letters.

5. *Games and Other Activities.*   Many games are outlined in *WTW EL* that will help you use the sort cards for vocabulary and language development activities. Variations of the Follow the Path game work especially well with beginning sounds.

Literature Connection

As you read books with your students, take time to introduce new vocabulary and compare the sounds of words. Find bilingual alphabet books or stories that feature letter sounds that are similar in English and Spanish, such as the following:

Ayala, L., & Isona-Rodriguez, M. (1995). *Los niños alfabéticos.* Watertown, MA: Charlesbridge Publishing.

Bridwell, N. (1984). *Clifford's family*. New York: Scholastic. Spanish edition available from Lectorum Publishers.

Elya, S. M. (2006). *F is for fiesta.* New York: Putnam Juvenile.

Garza, C. L. (2005). *Family pictures, 15th anniversary edition/Cuadros de familia, edición quinceañera.* San Francisco: Children's Book Press.

Hoberman, M. A. (2003). *Miss Mary Mack: A hand-clapping rhyme.* New York: Little Brown Company.

Miranda, A. (2001). *Alphabet fiesta.* New York: Turtle Books.

Priddy, R. (2005). *My little word book.* New York: Priddy Books.

Reiser, L. (1996). *Margaret and Margarita/Margarita y Margaret.* New York: Rayo Publications.

Rosa-Mendoza, G. (2000). *The alphabet/El alfabeto* (English and Spanish Foundation Series, Book 1). Wheaton, IL: Me+Mi Publishing.

Demonstrate, Sort, Check, and Reflect

(See page 24.)

1. Prepare a set of pictures to use for teacher-directed modeling. Use the letter/picture cards as headers and display the pictures randomly with picture side up. Learn the vocabulary of the pictures, as described in the standard weekly routines on pages 19–20. Place the three header cards on the table and make sure that students know their names.

2. Begin a **sound sort** by modeling one word into each column explaining explicitly what you are doing: *Here is a picture of a map.* Map *starts with the /m/ sound made by the letter* m *so I will put it under the picture of the mask. This is a picture of a Six. Ssssix starts with the /s/ sound made by the letter* s *so I will put it under the picture of the sun.* Model a picture under *p* in the same manner and then say: *Now who can help me sort the rest of these pictures?* Continue with the children's help to sort all of the pictures. Let mistakes go for now. If students say the name of the word in Spanish, congratulate them and repeat the English label. Discuss whether the word would go into the same column if you were doing it in Spanish. Your sort will look something like the one shown on page 21.

3. When all the pictures have been sorted, read each picture in the columns and check for any that need to be changed: *Do all of these sound alike at the beginning? Do we need to move any?*

4. Repeat the sort with the group again. Keep the letter cards as headers. You may want to mix up the words and turn them face down in a deck this time and let children take turns drawing a card and sorting it in the correct column. You can also simply pass out the pictures and have children take turns sorting them. After sorting, model how to check by naming the words in each column and then talk about how the words in each column are alike.

5. Give each student a copy of the sort for individual practice. Assign them the task of cutting out the pictures and then sorting on their own in the same way they did in the group. Give each student a plastic bag or envelope to store the pieces. On subsequent days, students should repeat the sorting activity several times. Involve the students in the other weekly routines listed on pages 19–20 and described in *WTW EL* for the letter name–alphabetic stage (Chapter 5).

6. Informally assess students on the feature under study throughout the week. Observe students' accuracy and fluency in sorting, and their knowledge of the English vocabulary. At the end of the week, call out four of the words you have been working with, and ask students to write the letter that they hear at the beginning on a small whiteboard or notepaper.

Extend

Consider doing the sort in Spanish for students who are just beginning to speak English. Following is a list of words that will work in both English and Spanish in Sorts 6 to 9.

m	p	s
map/mapa	potato/patata	sun/sol
melon/melón	penguin/pingüino	soup/sopa
motorcycle/motocicleta	paper/papel	salt/sal
mask/máscara	pajamas/piyama	six/seis
mom/mamá	pineapple/piña	saw/serrucho
mountain/montaña	park/parque	
	pear/pera	

n	f	g
nose/naríz	fire/fuego	goose/ganso
nut/nuez	family/familia	gas/gasolina
nine/nueve	football/fútbol	
night/noche		
numbers/números		

k	l	t
	lettuce/lechuga	tomato/tomate
	lemon/limón	tea/té
	lake/lago	television/televisión
	lion/león	tiger/tigre
	lip/labio	taxi/taxi
	letters/letras	
	light/luz	

c	y	b
car/carro	yogurt/yogur	button/botón
cut/cortar	yoyo/yoyo	boot/bota
calendar/calendario	yard/yarda	bike/bicicleta
camera/cámara		baby/bebé
cave/cueva		bat/bate
computer/computadora		bath/baño
cook/cocinero		bib/babero
cube/cubo		bus/(auto) bús

Completed sorts for this section are outlined in the following charts. Words in parentheses represent pictures.

Sort 6 Beginning Consonants: *m, p, s*

m (mask)	*p* (penguin)	*s* (sun)
(mountain)	(pineapple)	(salt)
(melon)	(pajamas)	(six)
(mom)	(park)	(soup)
(motorcycle)	(paper)	(saw)
(map)	(pear)	
	(potato)	

Sort 7 Beginning Consonants: *n, f, g*

n (nine)	*f* (fire)	*g* (goose)
(nut)	(father)	(game)
(night)	(foot)	(garden)
(nose)	(fish)	(girl)
(numbers)	(football)	(gum)
(four)	(family)	(gas)

Sort 8 Beginning Consonants: *k, l, t*

k (key)	*l* (lion)	*t* (turtle)
(kangaroo)	(lake)	(television)
(king)	(lip)	(telephone)
(kitchen)	(lemon)	(tent)
(kick)	(letter)	(taxi)
	(lettuce)	(ten)
		(tiger)

Sort 9 Beginning Consonants: *c, y, b*

c (car)	*y* (yard)	*b* (bike)
(camera)	(yoyo)	(book)
(cut)	(yogurt)	(bath)
(computer)	(yell)	(boy)
(calendar)		(baby)
(cave)		(bib)
		(boot)
		(bus)

SPELL CHECK 1   ASSESSMENT OF BEGINNING CONSONANTS WITH SIMILAR SOUNDS IN ENGLISH AND SPANISH

All the consonants from this section are assessed with Spell Check 1 on page 28. This is designed for use as a pretest and/or as a posttest. To administer the assessment, name each picture and encourage children to spell as much of the word as they can even though they will only be formally assessed on the initial sound. The pictures are:

1. lip	**2.** map	**3.** nut
4. gas	**5.** bat	**6.** key
7. lake	**8.** ten	**9.** cut
10. bus	**11.** pig	**12.** soup
13. foot	**14.** yell	**15.** gum

SORT 6   Beginning Consonants: *m*, *p*, *s*

SORT 7   Beginning Consonants: *n, f, g*

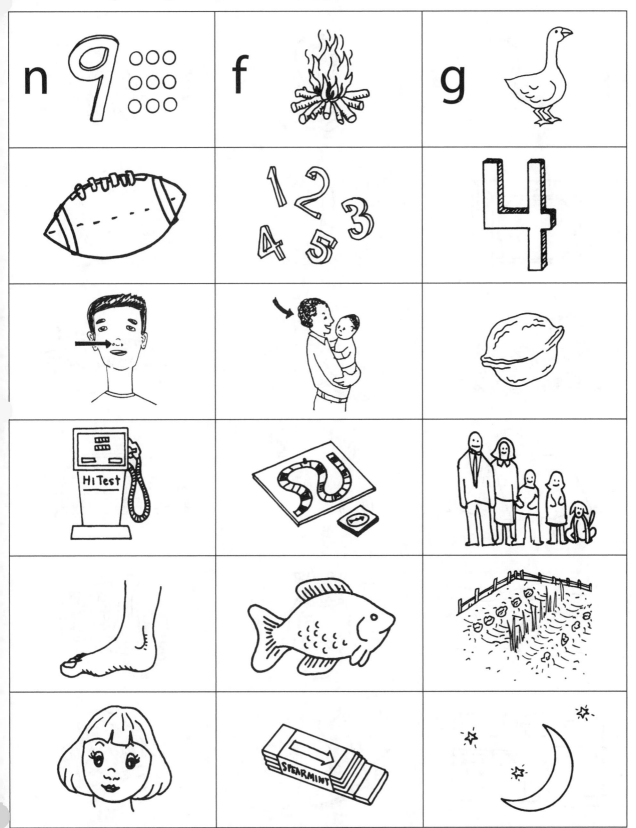

SORT 8   Beginning Consonants: *k, l, t*

SORT 9   Beginning Consonants: *c, y, b*

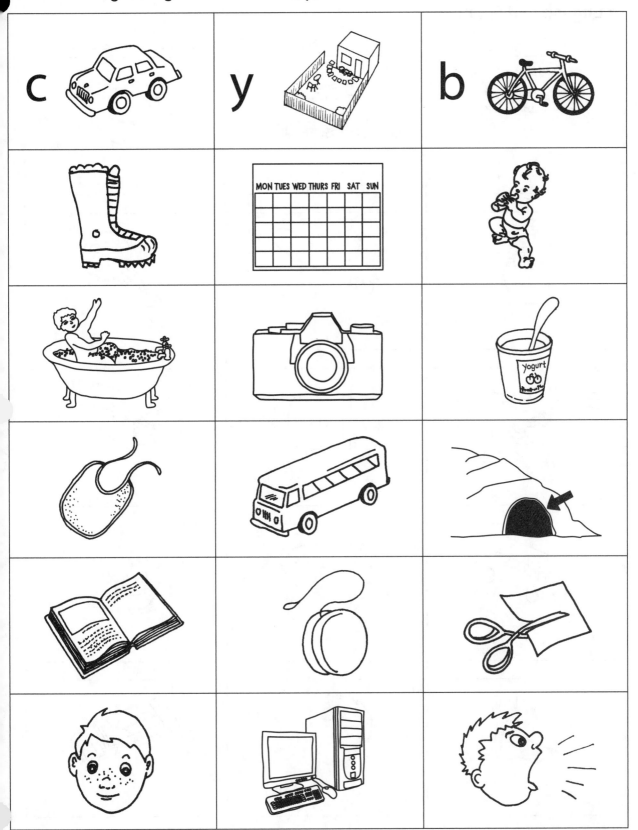

Spell Check 1   Assessment of Beginning Consonants with Similar Sounds in English and Spanish

Name _____

Unit III   Beginning Consonant Sounds That Are Distinct in Spanish and English

NOTES FOR THE TEACHER

These picture sorts continue to review the beginning consonants, and give you information about your students' letter sound knowledge. This second set of beginning consonant sorts features letters that have distinct sounds in English and Spanish. Each sort introduces two consonants that have a different sound in English and in Spanish, along with one consonant that is not different and was previously practiced. Because students may bring knowledge from previous schooling or home literacy experiences in Spanish, they may find these letter sound correspondences more difficult. These sorts provide an opportunity for you to assess your students' knowledge of initial consonants, as well as identify sounds that may be difficult for your students to distinguish and identify.

English learners in the letter name–alphabetic stage may confuse letter sound matches because the name of the letter suggests a different sound. This is true for *y* (wie) whose name begins with a /w/ sound, *g* (jee) which begins with /j/, and *h* (aich) which does not have the /h/ sound. Other confusions arise over sounds that are articulated similarly such as p/b, t/d, f/v, g/k. Spanish speakers may have confusions based on the similarities and differences of the letter sounds and names in English and Spanish; for example, the letter *j* makes a /j/ sound in English, a /h/ sound in Spanish. We have created sorts to contrast common confusions among Spanish speakers that you will find in the next section.

A review of beginning consonants is especially useful for first graders at the beginning of the year, and for all students in the early letter name stage. If students have missed only one or two consonants on a spelling inventory and you see that they are representing most consonants correctly in their writing, then a fast-paced review, doing a new sort every 3 to 4 days, may be all that is needed. Students who are still confusing many initial consonants probably need a slower pace, spending a week on each sort. If you identify specific letters or sounds that are confusing students, you can look to Sorts 14 to 18 for sorts that contrast problematic initial consonant sounds. You may want to use Spell Check 2 on page 38 as a pretest to see which children need a review of beginning consonants, and which consonants need to be reviewed.

Standard Weekly Routines for Use with Sorts 10–13

1. *Learn and Practice Unknown Vocabulary.*   Preview the pictures from the sort with your students. Name each picture, and have students repeat the name. Next, ask students to name the pictures. Set aside words that are unknown so they can be practiced. Select up to 10 of the unknown pictures for vocabulary study. Talk about the pictures with students, clarify their meanings, and invite students to use them in simple sentences. If possible, have students share the names of the pictures in their home languages.

2. *Repeated Work with the Pictures.*   Students should repeat the sort several times after it has been modeled and discussed under your directions. Make a copy of the black line master for each student, enlarging it to reduce paper waste and increase the size.

Provide opportunities for them to create their own categories for the sort, and to share their ideas with others. After cutting out the pictures and using them for individua. practice, the pieces can be stored in an envelope or plastic bag to sort again several times on other days. See *WTW EL* chapter 3 for tips on managing picture sorting.

3. *Draw and Label and Cut and Paste.* For seat work, students can draw and label pictures of things that begin with the target sounds/letters. They can also look for pictures in magazines and catalogs to cut out and paste into categories by beginning sound. The pictures from the black line sort can also be pasted into categories and children can be asked to label the pictures. This can serve as an assessment tool but *do not* expect accurate spelling of the entire word at this time.

4. *Word or Picture Hunts and Word Banks.* Students can look through their word banks, catalogs, and reading materials for words or pictures of things that have the targeted consonant sounds. Alphabet books are also a good place to look for additional words that begin with targeted sounds. Plan a time for students to share their findings. Words can be recorded on a group chart or students can create individual collages of cutout pictures that begin with the target letters.

5. *Games and Other Activities.* Many games are outlined in *WTW EL* that will help you use the sort cards for vocabulary and language development activities. Variations of the Follow the Path game work especially well with beginning sounds.

Literature Connection

Continue to share bilingual books with your students, and when possible compare the sounds that letters in Spanish make to those in English. Find rhythmic read-aloud stories that feature the sounds that are different between the two languages, such as those listed below. Encourage students to chant along during rereadings of the texts.

Ada, A. F. (2001). *Gathering the sun: An alphabet in Spanish and English.* New York: Harper Collins.

Appelt, K. (1998). *Bat jamboree.* New York: HarperTrophy.

Emberley, R. (1990). *My House: A book in two languages.* New York: Little, Brown.

Grande Tabor, N. M. (1993). *Albertina Anda Arriba: El Abecedario/Albertina Goes Up: An Alphabet Book.* Cincinnati, OH: AIMS International Books.

Kalman, M. (2001). *What Pete ate from A–Z (Really!)* New York: G. P. Putnam's Sons.

Lee, H. V. (1999). *I had a hippopotamus.* New York: Lee and Low Books.

MacDonald, R. (2003). *Achoo! Bang! Crash! The noisy alphabet.* Brookfield, CT: RoaringBrook Press.

Mora, P. (1999). *Confetti: Poems for children.* New York: Lee and Low Books. Spanish edition also available.

Pearson, D. (2003). *Alphabeep: A zipping, zooming ABC.* New York: Holiday House.

Raschka, C. (2003). *Talk to me about the alphabet.* New York: Henry Holt and Company.

Wolfe, F. (2001). *Where I live.* Plattsburgh, NY: Tundra Books. Spanish edition available from Editorial Juventud Publishers.

Demonstrate, Sort, Check, and Reflect

(See page 34.)

1. Prepare a set of pictures to use for teacher-directed modeling. Use the letter/picture cards as headers and display the pictures randomly with picture side up. Learn the vocabulary of the pictures, as described in the standard weekly routines on pages 29–30. Place the three header cards on the table and make sure that students know their names.

2. Begin a **sound sort** by modeling one word into each column as you explain what you are doing: *Here is a picture of a volcano.* Volcano *starts with the /v/ sound made by the letter v. Let's practice that sound /vvvvvvv/, it vibrates on your lip, doesn't it? Volcano sounds like* van *at the beginning, so I will put it under the picture of the van. This is a picture of a desk. Desk has a /d/ at the beginning, d-d-d-desk. I will put it under the picture of the dog.* Model a picture under *s* in the same manner and then say: *Now let's sort the rest of these pictures together.* Continue with the children's help to sort all of the pictures. Let mistakes go for now. If students say the name of the word in Spanish, congratulate them and repeat the English label. Discuss whether the word would go into the same column if you were doing the sort in Spanish. Your sort will look something like the one shown below.

3. When all the pictures have been sorted, read each picture in the columns and check for any that need to be changed: *Do all of these sound alike at the beginning? Do we need to move any?*

4. Repeat the sort with the group again. Keep the letter cards as headers. You may want to mix up the words and turn them face down in a deck this time and let children take turns drawing a card and sorting it in the correct column. You can also simply pass out the pictures and have the children take turns sorting them. After sorting, model how to check by naming the words in each column and then talk about how the words in each column are alike.

5. Give each student a copy of the sort for individual practice. Assign them the task of cutting out the pictures and then sorting on their own in the same way they did in the group. Give each student a plastic bag or envelope to store the pieces. On subsequent days students should repeat the sorting activity several times. Involve the students in the other weekly routines listed on pages 29–30 and described in *WTW EL* for the letter name–alphabetic stage.

6. Informally assess students on the feature under study throughout the week. Observe students' accuracy and fluency in sorting, and their knowledge of the English vocabulary. At the end of the week, call out four of the words you have been working with, and ask students to write the letter that they hear at the beginning on a small whiteboard or notepaper.

Completed sorts should resemble the following charts. Words in parentheses represent pictures.

Sort 10   Beginning Consonants: *v, d, s*

v (van)	*d* (dog)	*s* (sun)
(vase)	(desk)	(sad)
(vacuum)	(door)	(salt)
(violin)	(duck)	(seven)
(video player)	(dishes)	(seal)
(vest)	(doctor)	
(volcano)		

Sort 11   Beginning Consonants: *j, q, m*

j (juice)	*q* (queen)	*m* (mask)
(jet)	(quilt)	(mountain)
(jug)	(quack)	(money)
(jacket)	(quarter)	(motorcycle)
(jar)	(question)	(map)
(jump)		
(jeep)		
(jog)		

Sort 12   Beginning Consonants: *r, z, f*

r (rabbit)	*z* (zoo)	*f* (fire)
(refrigerator)	(zebra)	(father)
(rock)	(zero)	(fish)
(rain)	(zipper)	(four)
(roof)		(fence)
(ring)		(family)
(rat)		
(road)		

Sort 13   Beginning Consonants: *h, w, p*

h (hand)	*w* (window)	*p* (pig)
(house)	(worm)	(penguin)
(horse)	(wheel)	(paper)
(helicopter)	(wolf)	(park)
(heart)	(wig)	
(hill)	(web)	
(hat)		
(hammer)		

SPELL CHECK 2   ASSESSMENT OF BEGINNING CONSONANTS WITH DISTINCT SOUNDS IN ENGLISH AND SPANISH

Beginning consonants with distinct sounds in English and Spanish are assessed with Spell Check 2 on page 38. This is designed for use as a pretest and/or as a posttest. To administer the assessment, name each picture and encourage children to spell as much of the word as they can even though they will only be formally assessed on the initial sound. If students are representing some of the vowels and many final consonants, then they should be ready for the study of word families. If they are having difficulty distinguishing these sounds or representing them, the next chapter presents opportunities to contrast problematic beginning consonants. The pictures in the spell check are as follows:

1. van
2. queen
3. jet
4. rock
5. dig
6. hat
7. dog
8. zoo
9. wig
10. rain
11. jog
12. vase

SORT 10   Beginning Consonants: *v, d, s*

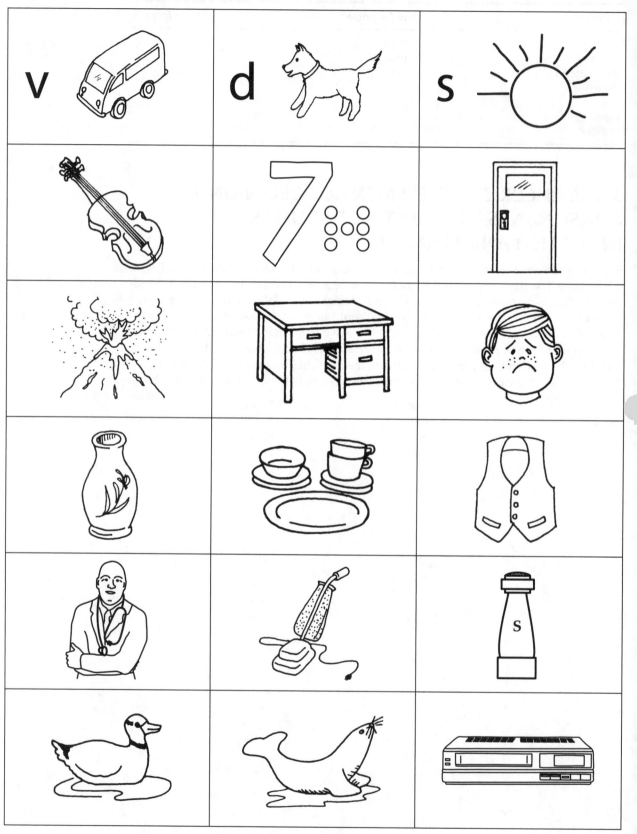

SORT 11   Beginning Consonants: *j, q, m*

SORT 12   Beginning Consonants: *r, z, f*

SORT 13   Beginning Consonants: *h, w, p*

Spell Check 2   Assessment of Beginning Consonants with Distinct Sounds in English and Spanish

Name _____

Unit IV   Beginning Consonant Sound Contrasts

NOTES FOR THE TEACHER

Unit II focused on common letter sound relationships between English and Spanish, and Unit III featured letter sound connections that are different between the two languages. Here we move along the continuum of difficulty by working with picture sorts that provide explicit opportunities for your students to focus on beginning consonant sounds that are sometimes the most difficult for Spanish speakers. Each sort features two consonants that are close in sound to each other, and may be confused for English learners. For example, because the letters *v* and *b* in Spanish are pronounced similarly, students may pronounce words that begin with *v* and *b* in a similar manner; hence, they may have difficulty distinguishing and sorting pictures with these sounds. It is only with practice and support that students will come to understand the differences in how the pairs of sounds are produced. Remember to be positive and playful as students work with these sounds. Help them to notice the articulatory features of these pairs of sounds. For instance, the /b/ sound is a burst from the lips, whereas the /v/ is a tickly vibration. The difference between /s/ and /z/ is that the /z/ makes a vibration in the throat, and so forth.

   You will not necessarily work through each of these sorts with all of your students. Rather, they are designed to help you focus your instruction for students who have shown some confusion with these beginning consonants in their writing, or in the sorts of the previous two units. Spell Check 3 on page 49 may also be used as a preassessment guide in choosing the sorts most appropriate to your students' needs.

Standard Weekly Routines for Use with Sorts 14–18

Follow the standard weekly routines for Sorts 6 to 9 on pages 19–20. You will use more or fewer of these activities depending on the amount of practice and reinforcement students need with the material.

Literature Connection

Find playful ways to practice the beginning sound contrasts presented in this chapter with the use of fun and rhythmic read-along books. Encourage students to chant phrases such as "four fur feet" to help them get the feel of the sounds and compare them to the sounds of distinct consonants. The following books are examples of playful stories and poems that can be used for this purpose.

Brown, M. W. (1996). *Four fur feet.* New York: Hyperion.

Carle, E. (2005). *Does a kangaroo have a mother, too?* New York: HarperTrophy.

Galdone, P. (1985). *Cat goes fiddle-i-fee.* New York: Clarion Books.

Parker, V. (1997). *Bearobics.* New York: Viking Juvenile.

Seuss, D. (1969). *I can lick 30 tigers today! and Other stories* (classic Seuss). New York: Random House.

Westcott, N. B. (1988). *The lady with the alligator purse.* New York: Little, Brown Young Readers.

Yee, W. H. (1996). *Big black bear.* New York: Houghton Mifflin.

Demonstrate, Sort, Check, and Reflect

(See page 44.)

1. Prepare a set of pictures to use for teacher-directed modeling. Use the letter/ picture cards as headers and display the pictures randomly with picture side up. Learn the vocabulary of the pictures, as described in the standard weekly routines on pages 19–20. Place the two header cards on the table and make sure that students know their names. For example, *Here is a picture of a fire next to the letter* f, *and a van next to the letter* v. *We will look for other things that start like* fire *and* van.

2. Begin a **sound sort** by modeling one word into each column as you explain what you are doing: Fire *and* van *sound a lot alike at the beginning, don't they? Sometimes it is hard to hear the difference, and we may get mixed up when we try to write those sounds. Let's say* f-f-f-fire *and* v-v-v-van. *Can you hear and feel the difference at the beginning of those words?* Help students say the sounds as needed to distinguish their features. *Let's look at some pictures to see if they sound more like* fire *or* van *at the beginning. Here is a picture of a family.* Family *starts with the /f/ sound made by the letter* f *so I will put it under the picture of the fire. This is a picture of a volcano.* V-v-v-volcano *starts with the /v/ sound made by the letter* v *so I will put it under the picture of the van.* Check to see that students are correctly articulating the /f/ and /v/ sounds. *Now let's sort the rest of these picture together.* Continue with the children's help to sort all of the pictures. Let mistakes go for now. Your sort will look something like the one shown on page 41.

3. When all the pictures have been sorted, read each picture in the first column and check for any that need to be changed: *Do all of these sound alike at the beginning? Do we need to move any?* Next, do the same in the other column.

4. Repeat the sort with the group again. Keep the letter/picture cards as headers. You may want to mix up the words and turn them face down in a deck this time and let children take turns drawing a card and sorting it in the correct column. You can also simply pass out the pictures and have the children take turns sorting them. After sorting, model how to check by naming the words in each column and then talk about how the words in each column are alike.

5. Give each student a copy of the sort for individual practice. Assign them the task of cutting out the pictures and then sorting on their own in the same way they did in the group. On subsequent days students should repeat the sorting activity several times. Involve the students in the other weekly routines listed on pages 19–20 and described in *WTW EL* Chapter 5.

6. Informally assess students on the feature under study throughout the week. Observe students' accuracy and fluency in sorting, and their knowledge of the English vocabulary. At the end of the week, call out four of the words you have been working with, and ask students to write the letter that they hear at the beginning on a small whiteboard or notepaper.

Extend

If you find that your students have difficulty distinguishing other beginning consonant sounds, you might want to prepare additional sorts that contrast the letters or sounds they are confusing. There are pictures and a template available in *WTW EL* to use for this purpose.

All sorts in this section should follow a similar procedure. The completed sorts should resemble the following charts. Words in parentheses represent pictures.

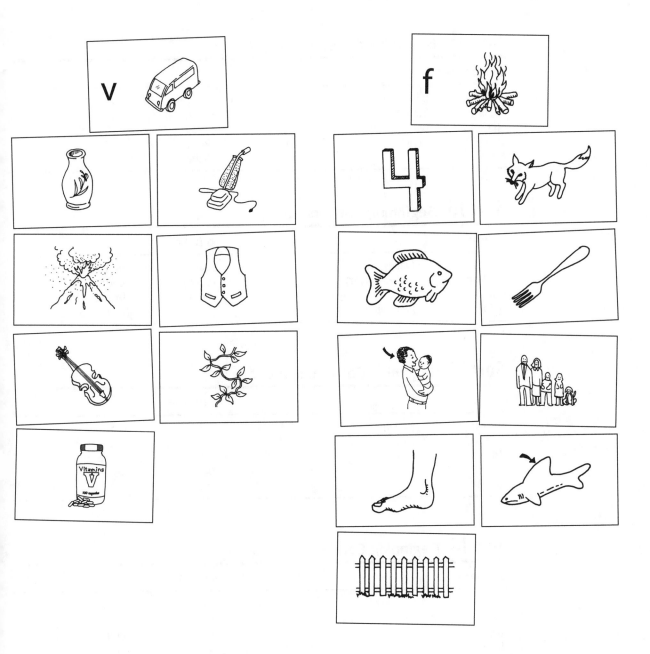

Sort 14 Beginning Consonants: *f, v*

f (fire)		*v* (van)	
(fence)	(fish)	(violin)	(vest)
(family)	(foot)	(vacuum)	(vase)
(father)	(fox)	(vine)	
(four)	(fork)	(volcano)	
(fin)		(vitamins)	

Sort 15   Beginning Consonants: *g, k*

g (goose)		*k* (key)	
(game)	(girl)	(kangaroo)	(kite)
(gum)	(garden)	(king)	(kitten)
(goat)	(gas station)	(kitchen)	
(gate)	(golf)	(kick)	
(gas)		(ketchup)	

Sort 16   Beginning Consonants: *v, b*

v (van)		*b* (bike)	
(vine)	(vase)	(bath)	(bib)
(volcano)	(video player)	(baby)	(bed)
(vest)	(vacuum)	(book)	(bus)
(violin)	(vitamins)	(bell)	(boy)

Sort 17   Beginning Consonants: *d, t*

d (dog)		*t* (turtle)	
(duck)	(desk)	(tub)	(top)
(dishes)	(dig)	(tie)	(television)
(deer)		(two)	(tiger)
(dive)		(towel)	(tag)
(doll)		(tire)	

Sort 18   Beginning Consonants: *z, s*

z (zoo)	*s* (sun)	
(zebra)	(six)	(soup)
(zero)	(saw)	(salt)
(zip)	(soap)	(sad)
(zigzag)	(seal)	(suit)
(zipper)	(sink)	(sandals)
	(socks)	

SPELL CHECK 3   ASSESSMENT OF BEGINNING CONSONANT CONTRASTS

Beginning consonant contrasts are assessed with Spell Check 3 on page 49. This is designed for use as a pretest and/or as a posttest. To administer the assessment, name each picture and encourage children to spell as much of the word as they can even though they will only be formally assessed on the initial sound. If students are representing the contrasting sounds correctly, then they probably do not need more focused work in this area. If they continue to have difficulty distinguishing these sounds or representing them, then more in-depth work is necessary. The pictures in Spell Check 3 are as follows:

1. bike
2. dig
3. sad
4. fin
5. vase
6. gate
7. tag
8. zip
9. gum
10. vine
11. dive
12. kite

SORT 14   Beginning Consonants: *f, v*

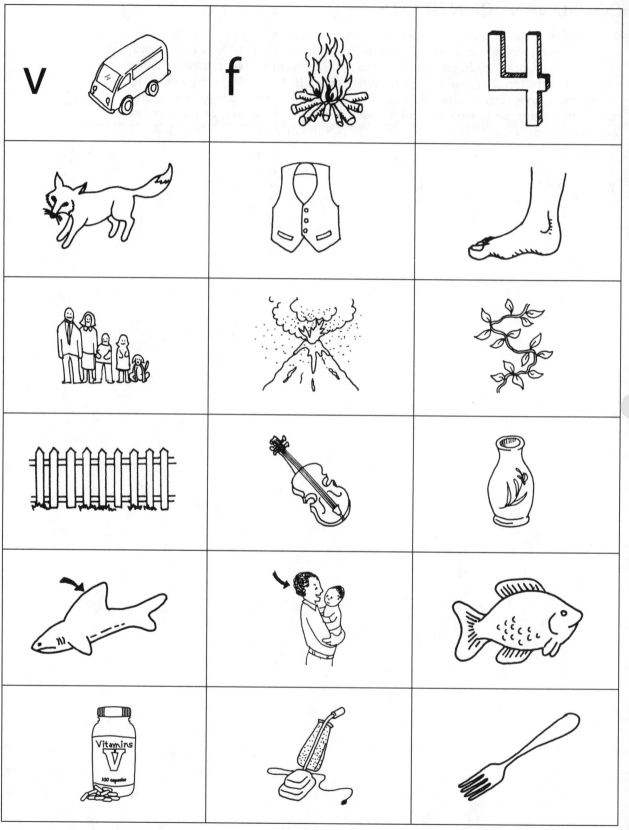

SORT 15   Beginning Consonants: *g, k*

SORT 16   Beginning Consonants: *v, b*

v	b	

SORT 17   Beginning Consonants: *d*, *t*

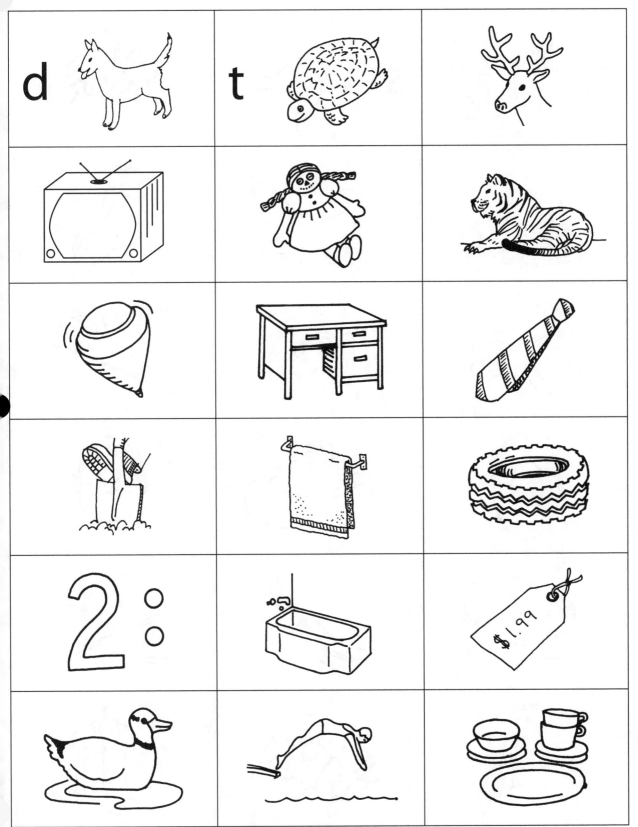

SORT 18   Beginning Consonants: z, s

Spell Check 3   Assessment of Beginning Consonant Contrasts

Name _____

Unit V Beginning Consonant Digraphs and Blends

NOTES FOR THE TEACHER

These picture sorts provide explicit opportunities for your students to focus on beginning consonant digraphs and blends, and compare them to the consonant sounds that are related visually. For example, Sort 19, which introduces the digraph *ch*, compares the /ch/ sound to /c/ and /h/. Sort 23 introduces the *st* blend, and compares its sound to objects that begin with /s/ or /t/. The final five sorts in this series work with the beginning sounds of digraphs and blends with contrasts that are difficult for Spanish speakers to hear. For example, Sort 30 addresses the slight difference between the /ch/ and /sh/ sounds that many Spanish speakers experience as challenging. Because there is not a /sh/ sound in many dialects of Spanish, students may have difficulty distinguishing and sorting pictures with these sounds. It is only with practice and support that students will come to understand the differences in how the pairs of sounds are produced. Remember to be positive and playful as students work with these sounds. Help them to notice the articulatory features of these pairs of sounds. For instance, the /ch/ sound is a burst from the mouth, whereas the /sh/ is a steady push of air. Students may want to add an *e-* in front of words that begin with the consonant blend *st* such as "estamp." This is natural, and should not be overly scrutinized or students will feel self-conscious. With practice and time, students will refine their sensitivity to the standard pronunciation.

You will not necessarily work through each of these sorts with all of your students. Rather, they are designed to help you focus your instruction for students who have shown some confusion with these beginning digraphs and blends in their reading or writing. Spell Checks 4 and 5 on pages 74–75 should be used as a preassessment guide in choosing the sorts most appropriate to your students' needs.

Standard Weekly Routines for Use with Sorts 19–34

Follow the standard weekly routines for Sorts 6 to 9 on pages 19–20. You will use more of these activities depending on the amount of practice and reinforcement students need with the material.

Literature Connection

Find playful ways to practice the beginning sounds presented in this chapter with the use of fun and rhythmic read-along books. Encourage students to chant phrases such as "chicka chicka boom boom" to help them get the feel of the sounds and match them to their spellings. The following books are examples of playful stories, songs, and poems that can be used for this purpose. You will notice many more in your classroom libraries!

Bryan, A. (2007). *Let it shine.* New York: Atheneum Books for Young Readers.

Cotton, C. (2007). *Some babies sleep.* New York: Philomel Books.

Fox, M. (2004). *Where is the green sheep?* San Diego: Harcourt.

Martin, B., & Archambault, J. (1989). *Chicka chicka boom boom.* New York: Simon & Schuster.

Shaw, N. (1997). *Sheep in a jeep.* New York: Houghton Mifflin.

Tafuri, N. (2007). *The busy little squirrel.* New York: Simon and Schuster.

Demonstrate, Sort, Check, and Reflect

(See page 58.)

1. Prepare a set of pictures to use for teacher-directed modeling. Use the letter/picture cards as headers and display the pictures randomly with picture side up. Learn the vocabulary of the pictures, as described in the standard weekly routines on pages 19–20. Place the header cards on the table and make sure that students know their names. For example, *Here is a picture of a chair next to the letters* ch, *a cat next to the letter* c, *and a hand next to the letter* h. Ch *are two letters put together to make one sound* /ch/. *We will look for other things that start like* chair, cat, *and* hand.

2. Begin a **sound sort** by modeling one word into each column as you explain what you are doing: *Here is a picture of a chimney.* Chimney *starts with the* /ch/ *sound made by the letters* ch. *Let's practice that sound ch-ch-ch, it pushes out of your mouth, doesn't it?* Chimney *sounds like* chair *at the beginning, so I will put it under the picture of the chair. This is a picture of a cow.* Cow *has a* /c/ *at the beginning, c-c-c-cow. I will put it under the picture of the cat.* Model a picture under *h* in the same manner and then say, *Now let's sort the rest of these pictures together.* Continue with the children's help to sort all of the pictures. Let mistakes go for now. Your sort will look something like the one shown below.

3. When all the pictures have been sorted, read each picture in the columns and check for any that need to be changed: *Do all of these sound alike at the beginning? Do we need to move any?*

4. Repeat the sort with the group again. Keep the letter cards as headers. You may want to mix up the words and turn them face down in a deck this time and let children take turns drawing a card and sorting it in the correct column. You can also simply pass out the pictures and have the children take turns sorting them. After sorting, model how to check by naming the words in each column and then talk about how the words in each column are alike.

5. Give each student a copy of the sort for individual practice. Assign them the task of cutting out the pictures and then sorting on their own in the same way they did in the group. Give each student a plastic bag or envelope to store the pieces. On subsequent days students should repeat the sorting activity several times. Involve the students in the other weekly routines described in this book and in *WTW EL* in Chapters 3 and 5.

6. Informally assess students on the feature under study throughout the week. Observe students' accuracy and fluency in sorting, and their knowledge of the English vocabulary. At the end of the week, call out four of the words you have been working with, and ask students to write the letter that they hear at the beginning on a small whiteboard or notepaper.

Extend

If you find that your students have difficulty distinguishing the sounds of the beginning consonant digraphs and blends, you might want to prepare additional sorts that contrast the letters or sounds they are confusing. There are pictures and a template available in *WTW EL* to use for this purpose.

Completed sorts for this chapter should resemble the following charts. Words in parentheses represent pictures.

Sort 19 Beginning Digraph *ch*

ch (chair)	*Cc* (cat)	*Hh* (hand)
(chain)	(cow)	(house)
(chin)	(corn)	(hook)
(cheese)	(car)	(hat)
(chop)	(cup)	(horse)
(chimney)		
(check)		
(cherries)		

Sort 20 Beginning Digraph *th*

th (thumb)	*Tt* (turtle)	*Hh* (hand)
(thorn)	(towel)	(heart)
(thermometer)	(tire)	(horn)
(thinking)	(toes)	(house)
(thirteen)	(tent)	
(thermos)	(toothbrush)	
	(two)	
	(teacher)	

Sort 21 Beginning Digraph *sh*

sh (ship)	*Ss* (sun)	*Hh* (hand)
(shark)	(soap)	(hill)
(shave)	(suit)	(heart)
(shop)	(sink)	(hook)
(shirt)	(sandals)	(horse)
(sheep)	(socks)	
(shoe)		

Sort 22 Beginning Digraph *wh*

wh (whale)	*Hh* (hand)	
(wheelbarrow)	(helicopter)	(hot)
(wheel)	(hen)	(hay)
(whisker)	(hop)	(hammer)
(whistle)	(hat)	(hospital)
(whip)	(hose)	(helmet)
	(heart)	

Sort 23 Beginning Blend *st*

st (star)	*Ss* (sun)	*Tt* (turtle)
(stop sign)	(seal)	(tire)
(stick)	(saw)	(toes)
(stairs)	(soap)	(towel)
(stamp)	(soup)	
(stapler)	(seven)	
(stool)		
(stir)		

Sort 24 Beginning *s*-Blends

st (star)	*sp* (spider)	*sn* (snail)	*sk* (ski)
(stick)	(spear)	(snake)	(skunk)
(stem)	(sponge)	(snowman)	(skeleton)
(stairs)	(spill)		(skirt)
(stamp)	(spoon)		(skate)

Sort 25 More Beginning *s*-Blends

sc (scarf)	*sm* (smile)	*sl* (slide)	*sw* (swing)
(scoop)	(smoke)	(sleeve)	(sweater)
(scale)	(smell)	(sleep)	(sweep)
(scout)		(sled)	(switch)
(scarecrow)		(slipper)	(swim)

Sort 26 Beginning *l*-Blends

cl (clouds)	*pl* (plug)	*fl* (flower)
(clock)	(plate)	(flag)
(closet)	(plant)	(flashlight)
(clipboard)	(plane)	(fly)
(claw)	(plus)	(float)
(clown)		
(climb)		
(clothes)		

Sort 27 More Beginning *l*-Blends

sl (slide)	*bl* (block)	*gl* (glue)
(sleeve)	(blouse)	(glasses)
(sleep)	(blender)	(globe)
(slipper)	(blindfold)	(glove)
(slip)	(blade)	(glass)
(sled)	(blow)	
	(blanket)	

Sort 28 Beginning *r*-Blends

br (broom)	*cr* (crab)	*fr* (frog)	*dr* (drum)
(bridge)	(cry)	(fruit)	(drive)
(bride)	(crack)	(frame)	(dress)
(bricks)	(crayon)	(freezer)	
(brush)	(crown)		
(bread)			

Sort 29 More Beginning *r*-Blends

gr (grapes)	*pr* (present)	*tr* (tree)
(grasshopper)	(prize)	(trap)
(graph)	(pretzel)	(trunk)
(grass)	(printer)	(tractor)
(grill)		(track)
(groceries)		(truck)
		(train)
		(triangle)

Sort 30 Beginning Digraphs: *ch, sh*

ch (chair)		*sh* (ship)	
(chop)	(cherries)	(shirt)	(shop)
(cheese)	(chin)	(shoe)	(sheep)
(chimney)		(shark)	(shell)
(check)		(shampoo)	(shelf)
(chain)		(shave)	

Sort 31   Beginning Sounds: *ch, y, j*

ch (chair)	*Yy* (yard)	*Jj* (juice)
(cherries)	(yell)	(jeep)
(chin)	(yoyo)	(jog)
(chain)	(yogurt)	(jump)
(chop)		(jet)
(cheese)		(jacket)
		(jug)
		(jar)

Sort 32   Beginning Sounds: *th, d, t*

th (thumb)	*Dd* (dog)	*Tt* (turtle)
(thermometer)	(door)	(telephone)
(thermos)	(dishes)	(teacher)
(thorn)	(duck)	(tent)
(thirteen)	(desk)	(ten)
	(doctor)	(taxi)
		(television)

Sort 33   Beginning Blends: *pr, br, gr, cr*

pr (present)	*br* (broom)	*gr* (grapes)	*cr* (crab)
(prize)	(bread)	(grass)	(crack)
(printer)	(brush)	(grasshopper)	(cry)
(pretzel)	(break)	(groceries)	(crown)
	(bridge)		(crayon)

Sort 34   Beginning Blends: *pl, bl, gl, cl*

pl (plug)	*bl* (block)	*gl* (glue)	*cl* (clouds)
(plane)	(blanket)	(glove)	(clown)
(plant)	(blouse)	(glass)	(claw)
(plus)	(blindfold)	(glasses)	(clock)
		(globe)	(clothes)

SPELL CHECKS 4 AND 5   ASSESSMENTS OF BEGINNING CONSONANT DIGRAPHS AND BLENDS

Beginning consonant digraphs are assessed with Spell Check 4 on page 74, and beginning consonant blends are assessed with Spell Check 5 on page 75. These assessments are designed for use as pretests and/or posttests. To administer one of the assessments, name each picture and encourage children to spell as much of the word as they can even though they will only be formally assessed on the initial sound or sounds. If students are representing the sounds correctly, then they probably do not need more focused work in this area. If they continue to have difficulty distinguishing these sounds or representing them, then more in-depth work is necessary. The pictures in the spell checks are as follows:

Spell Check 4

1. chin	**2.** soap	**3.** shut
4. cup	**5.** thumb	**6.** chop
7. wheel	**8.** toes	**9.** thorn
10. whale	**11.** sheep	**12.** thirteen

Spell Check 5

1. stem	**2.** prize	**3.** snail
4. blow	**5.** truck	**6.** crab
7. spill	**8.** plane	**9.** clap
10. swim	**11.** slip	**12.** braid
13. flag	**14.** grass	**15.** fry
16. dress	**17.** glue	**18.** smell

SORT 19   Beginning Digraph *ch*

SORT 20   Beginning Digraph *th*

SORT 21   Beginning Digraph *sh*

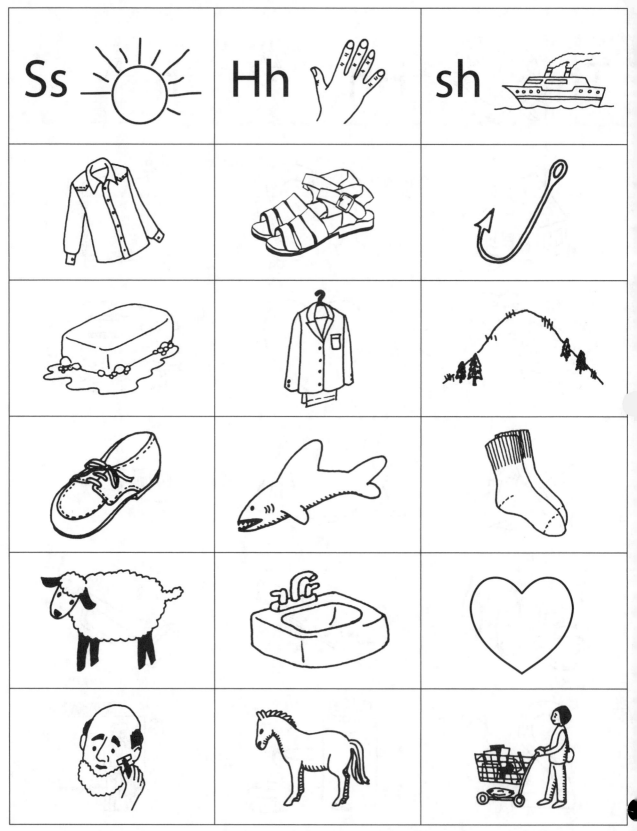

SORT 22   Beginning Digraph *wh*

SORT 23   Beginning Blend *st*

SORT 24   Beginning s-Blends

SORT 25 More Beginning s-Blends

SORT 26   Beginning *l*-Blends

SORT 27   More Beginning *l*-Blends

SORT 28   Beginning *r*-Blends

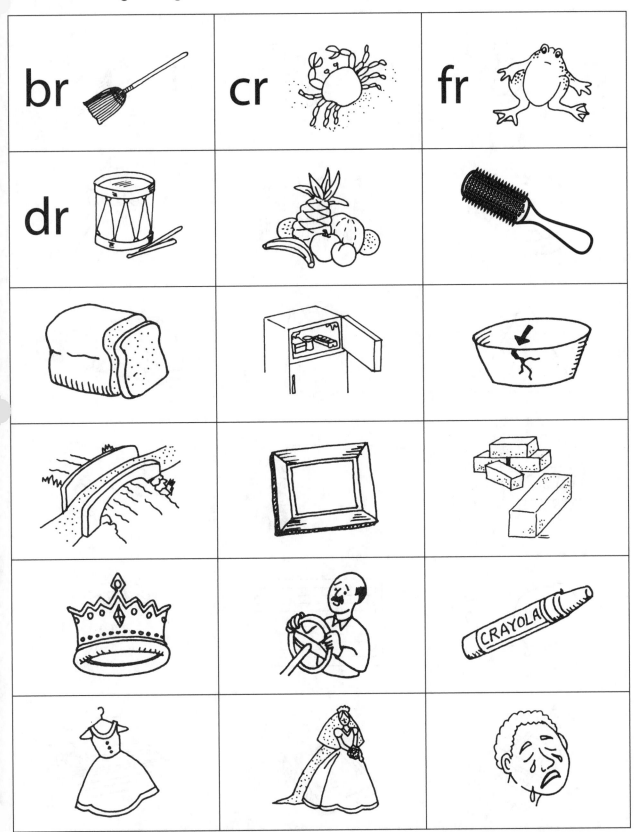

SORT 29   More Beginning r-Blends

SORT 30   Beginning Digraphs: *ch, sh*

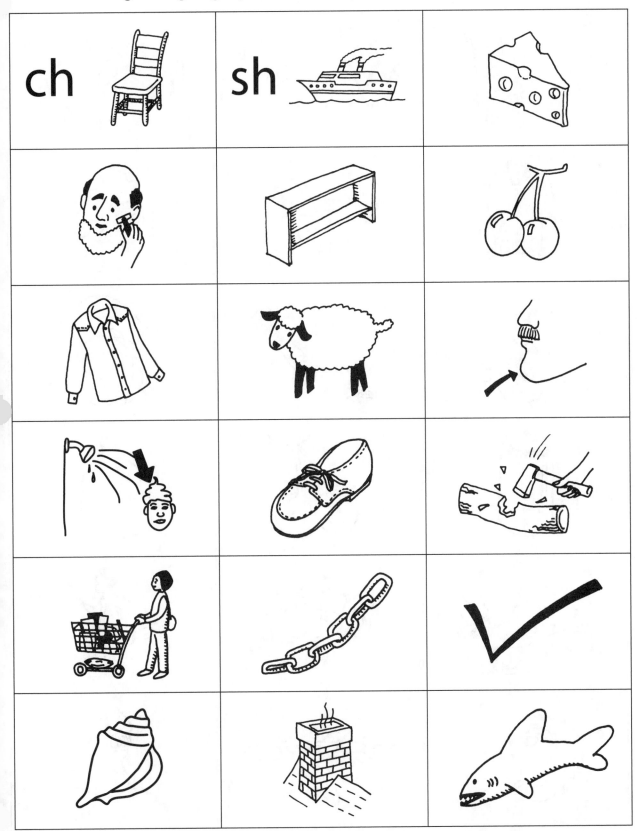

SORT 31   Beginning Sounds: *ch, y, j*

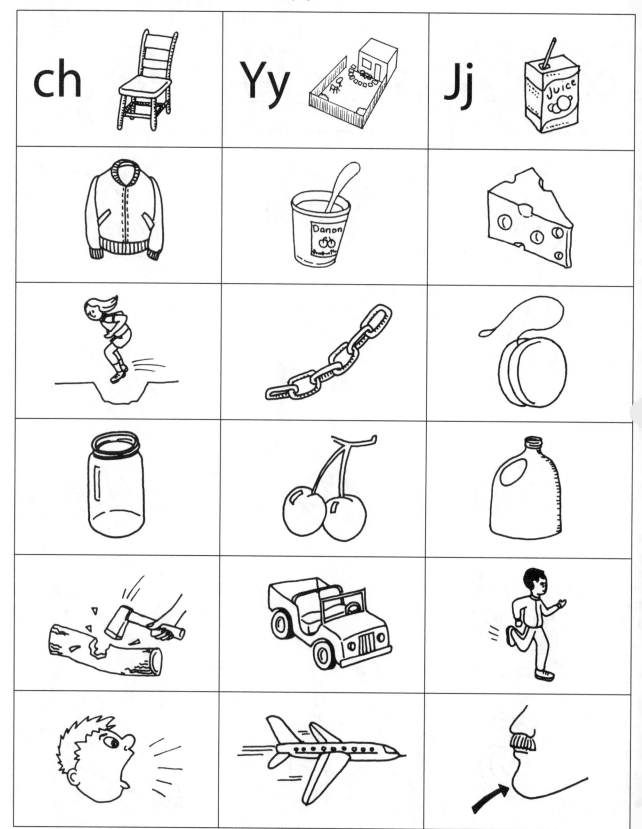

SORT 32   Beginning Sounds: *th, d, t*

SORT 33   Beginning Blends: *pr, br, gr, cr*

SORT 34   Beginning Blends: *pl, bl, gl, cl*

Spell Check 4   Assessments of Beginning Consonant Digraphs

Name _____

Spell Check 5   Assessments of Beginning Consonant Blends

Name _____

Unit VI   Listening for Ending Sounds

NOTES FOR THE TEACHER

These four picture sorts focus on ending sounds, and give you information about your students' ability to distinguish, as well as their accuracy in attaching the correct letter, for each sound. Most students learn the letter sound matches for final consonants along with initial consonants, and work with same-vowel word families helps to focus attention on final consonants. Once students develop the phonemic awareness to isolate and attend to final consonant sounds, the matches come easily. Students who lack this phonemic awareness or students whose native language does not have many final consonant sounds, as in Spanish, may need extra work with final consonants. Words in Spanish do not end with the same variety of consonants or consonant blends that they do in English. Spanish words can end with a vowel or *l, r, d, n*, or *s*. In contrast, most consonants in English are permitted to end words, and vowels at the end of words are much less common. For this reason, Spanish-speaking students sometimes have difficulty distinguishing ending sounds, and are known to add an extra vowel in their pronunciation or spelling of a word to make it "sound more correct." Each of these sorts introduces a set of pictures that ends with different sounds and gives you the opportunity to assess your students' abilities to discriminate their ending consonants. Use this information to provide tailored, explicit instruction that will help your students better understand the fine points of English alphabetic spelling.

A review of ending consonants is especially useful for first graders at the beginning of the year, and for all students in the early letter name stage. If students have missed only one or two consonants on a spelling inventory and you see that they are representing most consonants correctly in their writing, then a fast-paced review, doing a new sort every 3 to 4 days, may be all that is needed. Students who are confusing many ending consonants probably need a slower pace, spending a week on each sort. Use Spell Check 6 on page 85 as a pretest to see which children need a review of ending consonants, and which consonants need to be reviewed. To tailor additional sorts to the needs of your students, use the pictures and a blank template from the appendix of *WTW EL*.

Standard Weekly Routines for Sorts 35–38

Follow the standard weekly routines for Sorts 6 to 9 on pages 19–20. You will use more of these activities depending on the amount of practice and reinforcement students need with the material.

Literature Connection

Use simple picture books that feature playful rhymes or simple sentences with plenty of one-syllable words to help students practice saying words that end with a variety of ending consonants. Remember, students may want to drop the endings of words, so a shared reading or chanting along with a rhythmic phrase is the perfect opportunity to make those ending sounds feel more comfortable and natural to students. Here are a few examples to help you get started.

Banks, K. (2007). *Fox.* New York: Farrar, Straus & Giroux.

Casanova, M. (2007). *Some dog!* New York: Farrar, Straus & Giroux.

Seuss, D. (1960). *Green eggs and ham.* New York: Random House.

Seuss, D. (1965). *Fox in socks.* New York: Random House.

Thomas, J. (2007). *What will Fat Cat sit on?* New York: Harcourt Children's Books.

Willems, M. (2003). *Don't let the pigeon drive the bus!* New York: Hyperion.

Demonstrate, Sort, Check, and Reflect

(See page 81.)

1. Prepare a set of pictures to use for teacher-directed modeling. Use the letter/picture cards as headers and display the pictures randomly with picture side up. Learn the vocabulary of the pictures, as described in the standard weekly routines on pages 19–20. Place the header cards on the table and make sure that students know their names. For example, *Here is a picture of a bib next to the letter* b *and the word* bib, *a picture of gum next to the letter* m *and the word* gum, *and a bus next to the letter* s *and the word* bus. *In this sort we will be listening to the sound that we hear at the end of a word, not at the beginning. That's why there is a line before the letter, to show it is at the end. Look at the words* bib, gum, *and* bus. *They end with /b/, /m/, and /s/. We will look for other things that end like* bib, gum, *and* bus.

2. Begin a **sound sort** by modeling one word into each column as you explain what you are doing: *Here is a picture of a web.* Web *ends with the /b/ sound made by the letter* b. *Let's practice saying "web." Can you feel how the /b/ sounds at the end of the word?* Web *sounds like* bib *at the end, so I will put it under the picture of the bib. This is a picture of a drum.* Drum *has a /m/ at the end,* dru-mmm. *I will put it under the picture of the gum.* Model a picture under -s in the same manner and then say, *Now let's sort the rest of these pictures together.* Continue with the children's help to sort all of the pictures. Let mistakes go for now.

3. When all the pictures have been sorted, read each picture in the columns and check for any that need to be changed: *Do all of these sound alike at the end? Do we need to move any?*

4. Repeat the sort with the group again. Keep the letter cards as headers. You may want to mix up the words and turn them face down in a deck this time and let children take turns drawing a card and sorting it in the correct column. You can also simply pass out the pictures and have the children take turns sorting them. After sorting, model how to check by naming the words in each column and then talk about how the words in each column are alike.

5. Give each student a copy of the sort for individual practice. Assign them the task of cutting out the pictures and then sorting on their own in the same way they did in the group. Give each student a plastic bag or envelope to store the pieces. On subsequent days, students should repeat the sorting activity several times. Involve the students in the other weekly routines described in this book and in *WTW EL* Chapters 3 and 5.

6. Informally assess students on the ending sounds under study throughout the week. Observe students' accuracy and fluency in sorting, and their knowledge of the English vocabulary. At the end of the week, call out four of the words you have been working with, and ask students to write the letter that they hear at the beginning and the end on a small whiteboard or notepaper.

Extend

Using a variety of consonant cards or manipulative pieces such as *b, c, d, f, g, k, l, m, n, p, r, s, t* and *z*, have students play a guessing game with a partner. One person thinks of a simple word such as *map*, and the partner must find the beginning and ending consonants that go with the word (*m, p*). Partners trade off to see how many words they can think of and if they can find the letters to represent the sounds they hear.

Sort 35   Ending Sounds: /-b/, /-m/, /-s/

-b (bib) bib		-m (gum) gum		-s (bus) bus	
(web)	(tub)	(ham)	(drum)	(house)	(horse)
(crib)		(stem)	(mom)	(lips)	(gas)
(crab)		(dream)	(swim)	(socks)	

Sort 36   Ending Sounds: /-t/, /-p/, /-n/

-t (net) net		-p (mop) mop		-n (fan) fan	
(pot)	(hat)	(cup)	(soap)	(lion)	(sun)
(foot)	(bat)	(map)	(rope)	(moon)	(man)
(mat)		(top)		(ten)	

Sort 37   Ending Sounds: /-d/, /-f/, /-g/, /-r/

-d (bed) bed	-f (cliff) cliff	-g (dog) dog	-r (car) car
(add)	(knife)	(pig)	(fire)
(braid)	(roof)	(leg)	(four)
(lid)	(leaf)	(bag)	(star)
(road)		(rug)	

Sort 38   Ending Sounds: /-v/, /-z/, /-x/

-v (five) five		-z (prize) prize		-x (six) six
(dive)	(shave)	(hose)	(cheese)	(ax)
(cave)	(hive)	(nose)	(rose)	(fox)
(stove)	(drive)	(maze)	(toes)	(box)

Completed sorts for this chapter should resemble the following charts. Words in parentheses represent pictures.

SPELL CHECK 6   ASSESSMENT OF ENDING SOUNDS

Ending sounds are assessed with Spell Check 6 on page 85. This assessment is designed for use as a pretest and/or posttest. To administer the assessment, name each picture and encourage children to spell as much of the word as they can even though they will only be formally assessed on the initial sound and ending sounds. Be sure to clearly say the ending sound of each word, and look directly at students while dictating the words. Remember, students will be writing the sound they hear, not correctly spelling the word; for example, a correct response for *cave* would be CV. If students are representing the sounds correctly, they probably do not need more focused work in this area. If they continue to have difficulty distinguishing these sounds or representing them, more in-depth work is necessary. The pictures in the spell check are as follows:

1. tub	2. pet	3. gas
4. mom	5. cave	6. top
7. rug	8. ten	9. fire
10. maze	11. bag	12. leaf
13. box	14. lid	15. hat

SORT 35   Ending Sounds: /-b/, /-m/, /-s/

SORT 36   Ending Sounds: /-t/, /-p/, /-n/

SORT 37   Ending Sounds: /-d/, /-f/, /-g/, /-r/

SORT 38   Ending Sounds: /-v/, /-z/, /-x/

-v 5 five	-z 1st prize	-x 6 six

Spell Check 6   Assessment of Ending Sounds

Name _____

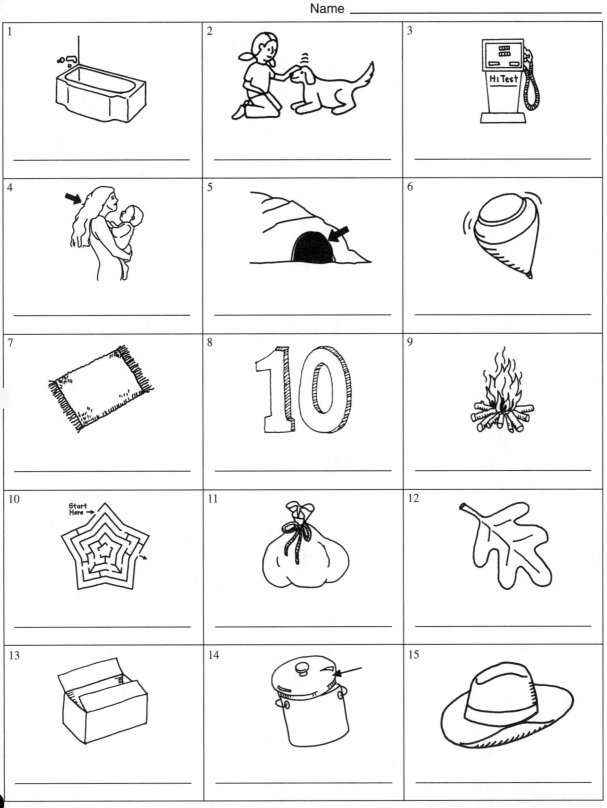

Unit VII   Vowel Sounds Picture Sorts

NOTES FOR THE TEACHER

These five picture sorts compare the long and short sound of each vowel, and give you information about your students' ability to distinguish these sounds. Spanish has only five vowels, and their spelling is highly consistent. Only one of the Spanish vowels has the same sound as a short vowel in English (short *o* with Spanish *a*). English learners may need help identifying and differentiating the variety of vowel sounds in English, especially because many of these sounds are not present in Spanish. These sorts are designed to provide many examples for students of the long- and short-vowel sounds, so that when they move into the upcoming short-vowel word family sorts, they have a solid oral foundation. Each of these sorts introduces a set of pictures representing the long and short sound of a particular vowel. Observe your students to gather information about their ability to differentiate these sounds. A formal spell check is not included in this chapter, because our work is with sounds only, not spelling.

Standard Weekly Routines for Sorts 39–43

Follow the standard weekly routines for Sorts 6 to 9 on pages 19–20 to reinforce these sorts. Because we are focusing on differentiating the short and long sounds of individual vowels, the most effective routines will be *learn and practice unknown vocabulary, repeated work with the pictures,* and *picture hunts.* Remember to focus on hearing the distinction between the short and long sound of a vowel, and not on how the word is written.

Literature Connection

Our study of short-vowel sounds during this chapter focuses on **hearing** the vowel sounds, so that students can identify the short-vowel families that will be presented in upcoming sections. For that reason, we suggest some playful games with vowel sounds. Many fun activities are presented in *Oo-pples and Boo-noo-noos: Songs and Activities for Phonemic Awareness* (Yopp & Yopp, 2003). Find those that help students interchange the vowel sounds of words, such as changing "I like to eat, eat, eat apples and bananas" to "I like to ot, ot, ot, opples and banonnos." Also, consider sharing short rhymes with students that feature a variety of words with short and long vowels so that they can compare the sounds they hear.

Hopkins, L. B. (2003). *A pet for me: Poems.* New York: HarperCollins.

Yopp, H. K., & Yopp, R. H. (2003). *Oo-pples and boo-noo-noos: Songs and activities for phonemic awareness.* New York: Harcourt School.

Demonstrate, Sort, Check, and Reflect

(See page 90.)

1. Prepare a set of pictures to use for teacher-directed modeling. Use the letter/picture cards as headers and display the pictures randomly with picture side up. Learn the vocabulary of the pictures, as described in the standard weekly routines on pages 19–20. Place the header cards on the table and make sure that students know their names. For example, *Here is a picture of a cat next to the letter* a, *and a picture of a train next to the letter* a. *In this sort we will be listening to the sound that we hear in the middle of a word, not at the beginning. Some words will have the sound like in the middle of* cat, *and others will have the sound like in* train. *We'll have to listen carefully to hear whether the words sound like* cat *or* train *in the middle.*

2. Begin a **sound sort** by modeling one word into each column as you explain what you are doing: *Here is a picture of a snake. Snake sounds like* train *in the middle. Let's practice saying "snake." Can you hear how it says /ay/ in the middle? Snake sounds like* train *in the middle, so I will put it under the picture of the train. This is a picture of a pan. Pan sounds like* cat *in the middle—caaaaat. I will put it under the picture of the cat.* Check to see that students are able to match the short *a* sound to the cat picture. *Now let's sort the rest of these pictures together.* Continue with the children's help to sort all of the pictures. Let mistakes go for now.

3. When all the pictures have been sorted, read each picture in the columns and check for any that need to be changed: *Do all of these sound alike in the middle? Do we need to move any?*

4. Repeat the sort with the group again. Keep the letter cards as headers. You may want to mix up the words and turn them face down in a deck this time and let children take turns drawing a card and sorting it in the correct column. You can also simply pass out the pictures and have the children take turns sorting them. Help student by stretching out the short and long *a* sounds of the header words as a review. After sorting, model how to check by naming the words in each column and then talk about how the words in each column are alike.

5. Give each student a copy of the sort for individual practice. Assign them the task of cutting out the pictures and then sorting on their own in the same way they did in the group. On subsequent days, students should repeat the sorting activity several times. Involve the students in the other weekly routines described in this book and in *WTW EL* for the letter name–alphabetic stage.

6. Informally assess students on the middle sounds under study throughout the week. Observe students' accuracy and fluency in sorting, and their knowledge of the English vocabulary.

Completed sorts for this chapter should resemble the following charts. Words in parentheses represent pictures.

Sort 39 Vowel Sounds: ă, ā

ă (cat)		ā (train)	
(flag)	(man)	(snake)	(rain)
(mask)	(hat)	(whale)	(skate)
(grass)	(bat)	(game)	(vase)
(pan)	(gas)	(plane)	(paint)

Sort 40 Vowel Sounds: ĭ, ī

ĭ (six)		ī (slide)	
(hill)	(lid)	(bride)	(five)
(bib)	(lips)	(knife)	(pie)
(fish)	(pig)	(kite)	(dive)
(wig)	(crib)	(bike)	(vine)

Sort 41 Vowel Sounds: ŭ, ū

ŭ (bus)		ū (glue)	
(gum)	(nut)	(tube)	(suit)
(mud)	(cut)	(cube)	(fruit)
(sun)	(bug)	(mule)	(two)
(hut)	(hug)	(flute)	(juice)

Sort 42 Vowel Sounds: ŏ, ō

ŏ (socks)		ō (soap)	
(mop)	(rock)	(stove)	(rose)
(box)	(top)	(bone)	(smoke)
(pot)	(clock)	(cone)	(coat)
(fox)	(dog)	(road)	
(dot)			

Sort 43 Vowel Sounds: ĕ, ē

ĕ (net)		ē (teeth)	
(hen)	(leg)	(beach)	(three)
(ten)	(bed)	(peas)	(peach)
(pet)	(egg)	(bee)	(bead)
(desk)	(vest)	(beak)	(feet)

ASSESSMENT OF VOWEL SOUNDS

Your assessment of the vowel sounds in this chapter will be informal. Your goal is to find out if students can distinguish between the short and long sound of each vowel. Consider jotting down notes on a clipboard as you watch students sort. Are they able to hear the differences in the vowel sounds, or are they asking others for help with each word? Students cannot be expected to fully master this differentiation before moving ahead with the short-vowel word families, but it will be important for you to know which students need extra auditory support as they become immersed in short-vowel word study.

informal

SORT 39   Vowel Sounds: ă, ā

SORT 40   Vowel Sounds: ĭ , ī

SORT 41   Vowel Sounds: ŭ, ū

SORT 42   Vowel Sounds: ŏ, ō

SORT 43   Vowel Sounds: ĕ, ē

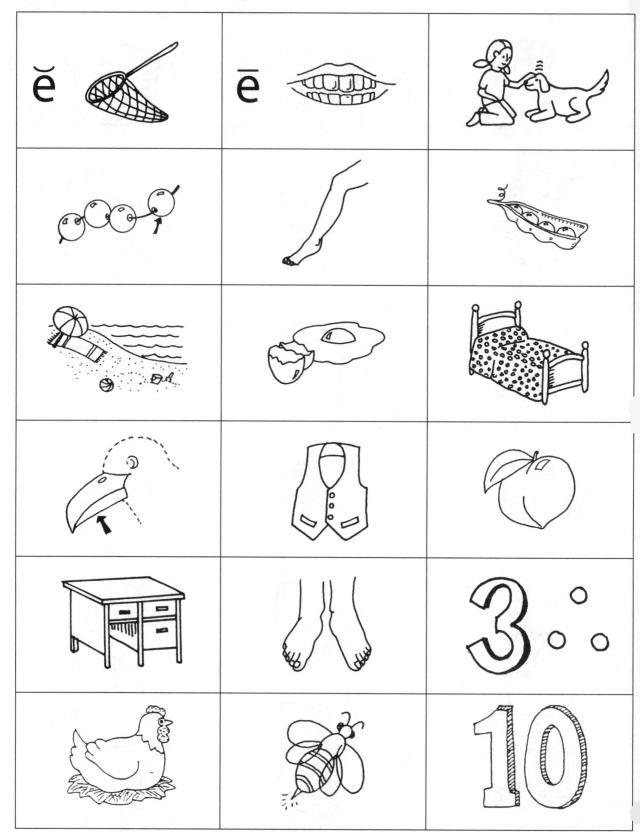

Unit VIII   Same-Vowel Word Families with Pictures

NOTES FOR THE TEACHER

The 15 sorts in this unit focus on word families of the same vowel, and contain an ever-increasing number of words and fewer pictures.

Word families or phonograms that share the same vowel are a good way to review consonants and introduce students to short vowels and the visual aspects of rhyme. While working with word families, children will practice phonological blending skills as they learn to say the **onset**, or first sound (such as the *c* in *cat* or the *fl* in *flat*), and add on the **rime** (the vowel and what follows, such as the *at* in *cat*) to figure out a word. This procedure should help English learners who have yet to master the skill of rhyming, because it not only simplifies the word choices but also offers textual support for seeing, not only hearing, the rhyme. This unit introduces same-vowel word families with the support of pictures. A later unit of mixed-vowel word families repeats many of these same families but with more limited picture support. Students will:

- Learn the meanings of words that will be useful for their beginning reading materials
- Sort pictures and words by rhyming sound and identify rhyming words
- Match words to pictures using beginning and ending consonant sounds
- Learn to isolate, identify, and blend the onsets and rimes in word families
- Read and spell words in families that contain the same short vowel

These sorts can be used with early letter name spellers who have nearly mastered consonants in the initial and final positions (spelling *fun* as FN or *mad* as MD) and may be including some medial vowels (as in BOT for *boat*). Initial and final consonants will be reviewed in these sorts, and blends and digraphs are included. Spell Checks 7 and 8 on pages 119–120 can be used as pretests as well as posttests. Students who score at least 90% can move on to other features.

There are 15 word family sorts in this section that feature words and pictures and focus on only one vowel at a time. In general, you will want to spend several days with each sort, implementing the standard weekly routines described next. We especially recommend *building, blending, and extending*. If you need to slow the pace, spend more time on each sort or focus on only one family at a time before comparing two families.

Standard Weekly Routines for Use with Word Families in Sorts 44–58

1. *Learn and Practice Unknown Vocabulary.* As in all of the previous sorts, it is important your students know the meaning of each picture or word in a sort. Preview the sort cards with your students to ensure they know what each item is. When there is a picture and word that match, have students pair them up. Ask students to name the pictures, and discuss any words that may be unfamiliar. Set aside words and pictures that are unknown so they can be practiced in vocabulary study. Talk about the pictures with students, clarify their meanings, and invite students to use them in simple sentences. If possible, have students share in Spanish to clarify the meaning of any unknown items.

2. ***Repeated Work with the Pictures and Words.***   Students should work with the featured sorts several times after the sort has been modeled and discussed. After cutting out the words and pictures and using them for individual practice, students can store the pieces in an envelope or plastic bag to sort again several times on other days. The pictures and words can also be used in partner activities during which children work together to read and spell the words. At some point children may glue the sort onto paper or keep it to combine with additional sorts in review lessons.

3. ***Building, Blending, and Extending.***   Students should be able to read and spell these words, so they should get practice doing both. This activity allows students to spell with manipulatives. Use the *building, blending, and extending* cards with onsets and rimes on pages 179 to 182 of this book for these activities. The cards can be enlarged for use in a pocket chart and can also be duplicated for use by individual students. Magnetic letters also work well but the rime unit should be kept together when working with word families.

   For *building*, say the word and then model how to make the word by putting together the onset and then the rime as shown here. Model how to change the onset to create other familiar words from the sort. Children can work with similar materials on their own or with a partner at their seats.

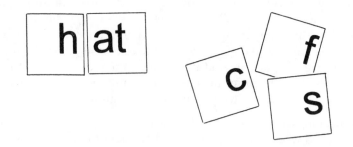

   For *blending*, place the onset and rime in a pocket chart or write them on the board. Say the onset and then the rime as slowly as possible without distortion (e.g., /ssss/ pause /aaaat/) pointing to the *s* and then the *at* as a unit. Then say the word naturally as you run your hand under it or push the cards together: *sat*. Model how you can change the onset to create a new word such as *mat*. Have the students say the sounds with you and then individually. Do not isolate the vowel and the final sound. Children should learn these as a unit at this point.

   For *extending*, include words in the blending activity from the list of additional words in each lesson. This will help students see that knowing a word family can help them figure out many additional words as well as the ones featured in the sort.

4. ***Reading.***   Use decodable texts or little books that have a number of words with the featured family. Many publishers are now creating "phonics readers," and some of them focus on word families. Be sure students can read these books with 90% accuracy on a second reading and understand the vocabulary. Screen the books for natural language patterns; stifled language such as, "Fan the pan, man!" will be difficult for English learners to make sense of because it does not sound like normal speech. It is important that we communicate how important comprehending the text is to students learning English, and that they learn to ask questions when things fail to make sense.

5. ***Word Recognition.***   After students have worked with the words and pictures for several days, hold up just the words and practice word recognition. Students can work in pairs to practice saying the words. Model blending of the onset and rime if students have trouble.

6. *Spelling.*   Hold up pictures one at a time and have the students spell the word using letter cards, chalkboards, whiteboards, or pencil and paper. Ask students to underline the letters (such as *ad*) that are the same in every word. Students can also work with a partner, taking turns calling a word for their partner to spell and then showing the word to check it.

7. *Word Hunts.*   Look for words in daily reading that mirror the featured word families. Challenge children to find others that could go in the family or brainstorm additional words, but understand that it may be difficult to find them. Beginning speakers of English will have fun creating rhyming words, but they may not always know whether they have created a "real word." Keep a list of rhyming words and have students discuss whether they are real words, "made-up" words, or if they don't know. Consider the following examples from the *-ad* word family: *bad, cad, dad, fad, gad, had, jad, kad, lad, mad, nad, pad, rad, sad, tad, vad, wad, yad,* and *zad.* Students may be quite confident about *bad, dad, had, mad,* and *sad* being real words, but they may truly be at a loss on less frequent words such as *cad* or *fad.* When a word is unknown but fairly common and useful, consider spending instructional time to learn it. Such might be the case with a word like *pad.* When possible, spend your precious instructional time working on the essential words to support meaningful oral language and early reading experiences.

8. *Games and Other Activities.*   Create flip books, Letter Slides, or Word Family Wheels like those described in *WTW EL* for students to reread words in each family.

9. *Assessment.*   To assess student's weekly mastery, ask them to spell and read the words. Students can be given a traditional spelling test because they are only working with a limited number of word families, or you can use whiteboards to dictate some of the featured words of the week. Have students number their paper or whiteboard and call aloud a sample of words from the lesson. Spell Checks 7 and 8 are included at the end of this section and can serve as post- or preassessments.

Literature Connection

To liven up your study of word families, find some simple rhyming books that use these words in funny or creative ways. Help students identify words that use the key word families you are studying. We offer a beginning list as follows:

Alborough, J. (2006). *Hit the ball Duck.* La Jolla, CA: Kane Miller Book Publishers.

Cole, J., & Calmenson, S. (1996). *Bug in a rug: Reading fun for just beginners.* New York: William Morrow & Co.

Florian, D. (2003). *Bow wow meow meow: It's rhyming cats and dogs.* New York: Harcourt Children's Books.

Freeman, D. (1988). *Pet of the Met.* New York: Puffin.

Grace, W., & Geist, K. (2007). *Three little fish and the big bad shark.* New York: Scholastic Cartwheel Books.

Karlin, N. (1998). *The fat cat sat on the mat* (I can read book 1). New York: Harper Trophy.

Kent, J. (1987). *The fat cat.* New York: Scholastic.

Langstaff, J. (1991). *Oh, a hunting we will go.* New York: Aladdin Paperbacks.

LaRochelle, D. (2004). *The best pet of all.* New York: Penguin Young Readers Group. Spanish edition available from Fondo de Cultura Económica USA.

Lewis, J. P. (2007). *Big is big (and little, little).* New York: Holiday House.

London, J. (2007). *My big rig.* Tarrytown, NY: Marshall Cavendish Corporation.

Wildsmith, B. (1987). *Cat on the mat.* Oxford: Oxford University Press.

Demonstrate, Sort, Check, and Reflect

(See page 104.) Prepare a set of pictures and words to use for teacher-directed modeling, such as for Sort 44: *at/ad*.

1. Introduce the pictures with a **rhyming sort.** Place the picture of the *cat* and the *dad* as headers for the sort (as shown below). Explain that the students need to listen for rhyming words and put them under the correct picture. Select another picture such as *hat*. Ask: *Does hat rhyme with cat or dad? Yes, it rhymes with cat so we will put it under the picture of the cat.* Continue until all the pictures have been sorted. Have the students join in as you name them from top to bottom. Ask the students how the words in each column are alike: *These words rhyme.* Leave the headers and remove the other pictures. Hand out the pictures or place them randomly to the side or in a deck. Call on children individually to help sort the words again by rhyme.

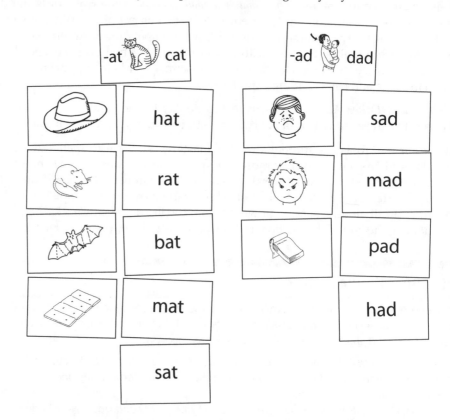

2. Next introduce the word cards. Arrange them randomly below or off to the side where everyone can see them. Name the first picture and ask if someone can find that word. *Can someone find the word hat? How did you know that word was hat? Yes it starts with an h and ends with a t.* Follow this procedure until all of the words that match a picture are done. If there are additional word cards, guide students to add the onset onto the word family it belongs to. Say, *Here is a word without a picture. It starts with h and ends with ad. What word is that?* Guide students to blend the word together *h-ad, had. Where should we put the word had in our sort?* Read down the list of words in one column at a time and ask how they are alike. Children should note that they rhyme and they end in the same two letters. Point out that students are learning about word families and in this sort they worked with the *at* and *ad* families.

3. Remove the words. Arrange them randomly, put them in a deck, or hand them out to children in the group to match back to the words. Encourage children to tell how they could do the matching and once more ask how the words are alike.

Extend

Make a copy of the sort for the students. Have them take the sort home to practice with their families. Do several of the standard weekly routines listed on pages 95–97 throughout the week.

Completed sorts for this chapter should resemble the following charts. Words in parentheses represent pictures. Additional words for the word families are listed below each sort.

Sort 44 Word Family: *at, ad*

-*at* (cat) cat		-*ad* (dad) dad	
(hat)	hat	(sad)	sad
(rat)	rat	(pad)	pad
(mat)	mat	(mad)	mad
(bat)	bat		had
	sat		

Additional Words. *at, that, fat, pat, flat, brat, chat, gnat, bad, rad, glad, lad*

Sort 45 Word Family: *ap, ag*

-*ap* (map) map		-*ag* (tag) tag	
(nap)	nap	(bag)	bag
(clap)	clap	(flag)	flag
(snap)	snap	(wag)	wag
	tap		rag
	lap		drag

Additional Words. *cap, gap, rap, yap, zap, flap, slap, trap, chap, wrap, sag, nag, brag, snag, lag, tag*

Sort 46 Word Family: *am, ab*

-*am* (ham) ham		-*ab* (crab) crab	
(dam)	dam	(cab)	cab
(clam)	clam		stab
	Sam		grab
	ram		scab
	jam		lab
	yam		
	slam		
	bam		

Additional Words. *am, cram, wham, swam, gram, dab, jab, nab, tab, blab, slab*

Sort 47 Word Family: *ag, ab, an*

-*ag* (tag) tag		-*ab* (crab) crab	-*an* (man) man	
(bag)		grab	(fan)	fan
	wag	cab	(van)	van
		lab	(can)	can
			(pan)	pan
				plan
				ran

Additional Words. *an, than, tan, scan*

Sort 48 Word Family: *ip, ig*

-*ip* (lip) lip		-*ig* (wig) wig	
(zip)		(pig)	pig
(clip)	clip	(dig)	dig
(ship)	ship		big
	dip		twig
	chip		
	rip		
	trip		
	drip		

Additional Words. *hip, nip, sip, tip, whip, flip, slip, skip, fig, rig, wig, zig*

Sort 49 Word Family: *ib, in, it*

-*ib* (crib) crib		-*in* (pin) pin		-*it* (sit) sit	
(bib)		(fin)	fin	(hit)	hit
	rib		tin		bit
	fib		thin		pit
			in		fit
			win		kit

Additional Words. *bin, twin, chin, shin, spin, grin, it, lit, wit, skit, spit, slit, quit*

Sort 50 Word Family: *id, ick, ill*

-*id* (lid) lid		-*ick* (sick) sick		-*ill* (hill) hill	
(kid)	kid	(kick)	kick	(pill)	pill
	hid	(stick)			still
	did	(chick)			fill
			pick		will
			lick		

Additional Words. *bid, rid, slid, skid, tick, slick, quick, trick, flick, brick, thick, click, prick, dill, kill, gill, mill, till, bill, drill, grill, chill, skill, spill*

Sort 51 Word Family: *ut, ug*

-*ut* (nut) nut		-*ug* (bug) bug	
(cut)	cut	(rug)	rug
(hut)	hut	(hug)	hug
	but	(plug)	
	gut		dug
	shut		tug
			mug
			snug

Additional Words.   rut, jut, jug, slug, drug

Sort 52 Word Family: *ub, um*

-*ub* (tub) tub		-*um* (drum) drum	
(cub)	cub	(plum)	plum
	rub	(gum)	gum
	stub		bum
	club		sum
	grub		hum
			chum
			scum
			strum

Additional Words.   hub, snub, slum

Sort 53 Word Family: *ud, up, un*

-*ud* (mud) mud		-*up* (cup) cup		-*un* (sun) sun	
(bud)	bud	(up)	up	(run)	run
	stud		pup	(bun)	bun
	dud				stun
	thud				gun
					fun

Additional Words.   spun

Sort 54 Word Family: *op, og*

-*op* (top) top		-*og* (dog) dog	
(mop)	mop	(frog)	frog
(chop)	chop	(log)	log
(stop)	stop		jog
	hop		fog
	pop		hog
	drop		

Additional Words.   cop, slop, flop, shop, crop, plop, prop, clog

Sort 55 Word Family: *ot, ob*

-*ot* (pot) pot		-*ob* (knob) knob
(cot)	cot	cob
(knot)		mob
	hot	job
	lot	rob
	got	sob
	not	bob
	spot	glob
		blob

Additional Words.   *jot, dot, rot, tot, clot, gob*

Sort 56 Word Family: *od, ock, oss*

-*od* (rod) rod	-*ock* (rock) rock		-*oss* (toss) toss	
pod	(clock)	clock	(cross)	cross
nod	(sock)			moss
clod		shock		loss
plod		lock		boss
sod				

Additional Words.   *prod, odd, dock, tock, block, flock, smock, stock*

Sort 57 Word Family: *et, en*

-*et* (net) net		-*en* (hen) hen	
(jet)	jet	(pen)	pen
	get	(ten)	ten
	bet		when
	yet		then
	wet		den
	met		men
	let		

Additional Words.   *pet, set, vet, fret*

Sort 58 Word Family: *ed, eg, ell*

-*ed* (bed) bed		-*eg* (leg) leg		-*ell* (bell) bell	
(sled)	sled	(peg)	peg	(shell)	
	led		keg		sell
	sped		beg		tell
	wed				
	bled				
	shed				
	red				

Additional Words.   *fed, fell, well, smell, spell, swell, dwell*

SPELL CHECKS 7 AND 8   ASSESSMENTS
OF SAME-VOWEL WORD FAMILIES

Same-vowel word families are assessed with Spell Checks 7 and 8 on pages 119 and 120. These assessments are designed for use as pretests and/or posttests. To administer one of the assessments, name each picture and have students circle the word that goes with the picture. Recognition rather than production is assessed at this point, as students have not yet contrasted short vowels. Students can also complete this task independently. If students are able to select words correctly, they probably do not need more focused work in this area. If they continue to have difficulty distinguishing the correct word families, more in-depth work is needed. The pictures in the spell checks are as follows:

Spell Check 7

1. hat	**2.** map	**3.** bib
4. fin	**5.** ship	**6.** sad
7. cab	**8.** hill	**9.** ham
10. dig	**11.** can	**12.** sit
13. kid	**14.** bag	**15.** kick

Spell Check 8

1. nut	**2.** dog	**3.** rod
4. mud	**5.** cot	**6.** rug
7. tub	**8.** sock	**9.** ten
10. gum	**11.** sob	**12.** bun
13. mop	**14.** cup	**15.** leg

SORT 44 Word Family: *at, ad*

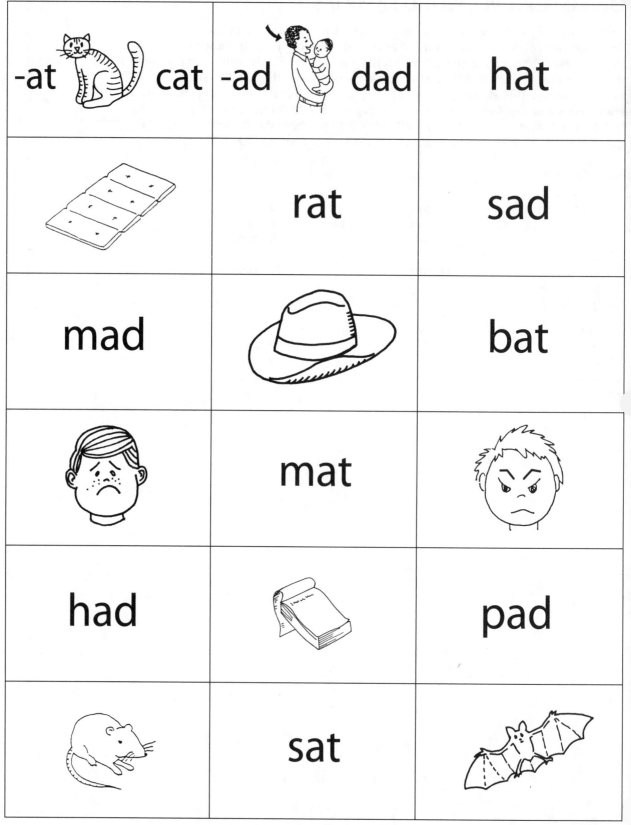

-at 🐱 cat	-ad 👨 dad	hat
	rat	sad
mad	🤠	bat
😟	mat	😠
had	📖	pad
🐀	sat	🦇

SORT 45   Word Family: *ap, ag*

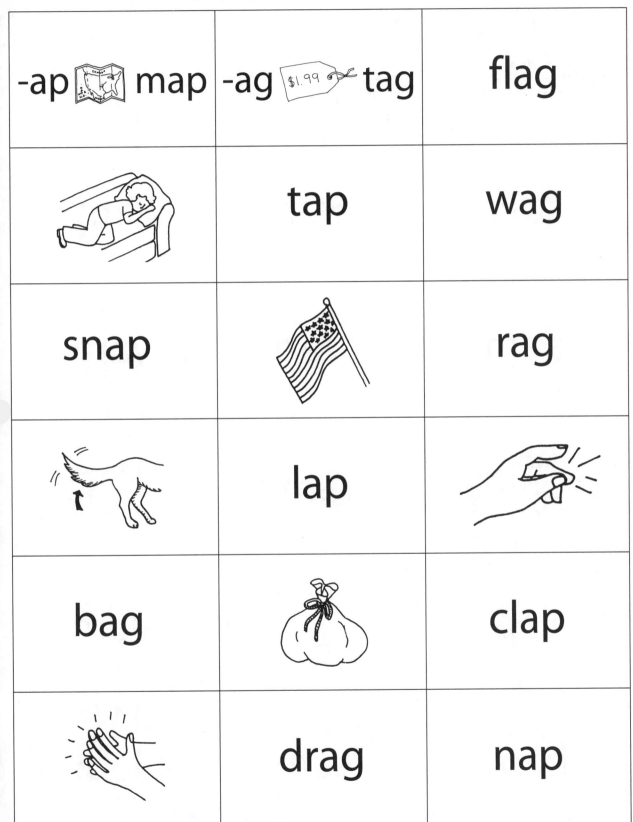

-ap map	-ag tag	flag
	tap	wag
snap		rag
	lap	
bag		clap
	drag	nap

SORT 46   Word Family: *am, ab*

-am  ham	-ab crab	Sam
stab	grab	jam
dam	scab	yam
(taxi)	ram	(clam)
cab	(dam)	slam
bam	clam	lab

SORT 47   Word Family: *ag, ab, an*

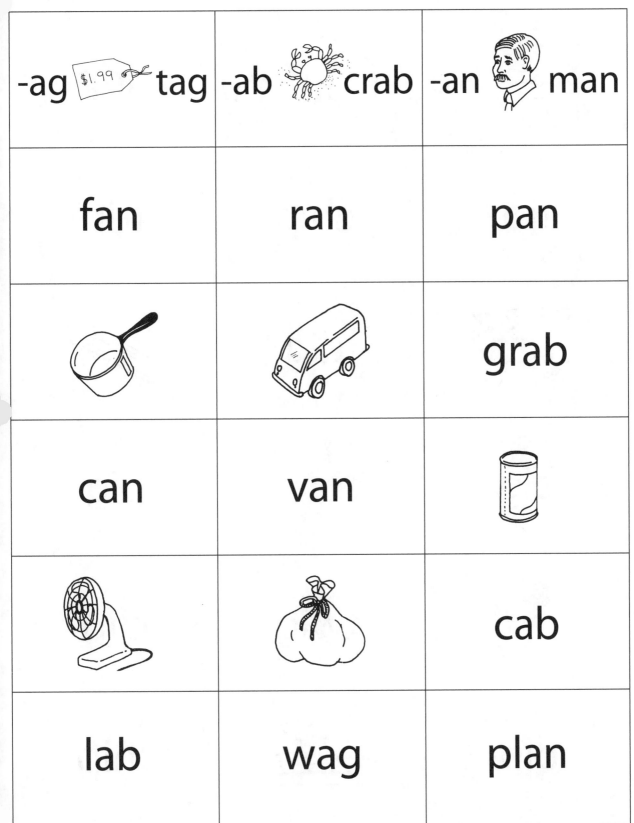

-ag $1.99 tag	-ab crab	-an man
fan	ran	pan
		grab
can	van	
		cab
lab	wag	plan

SORT 48   Word Family: *ip, ig*

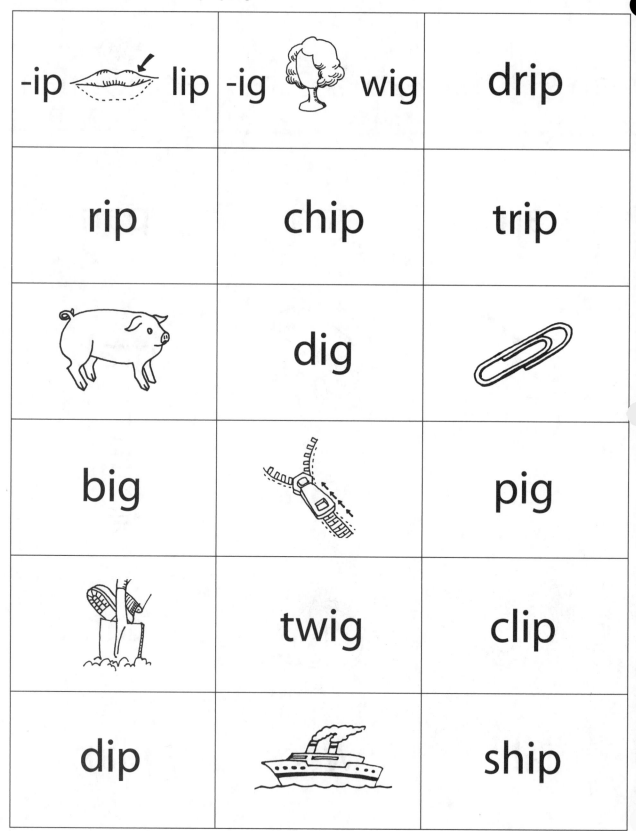

-ip 👄 lip	-ig 🌳 wig	drip
rip	chip	trip
🐷	dig	📎
big	🤐	pig
🥾	twig	clip
dip	🚢	ship

SORT 49   Word Family: *ib, in, it*

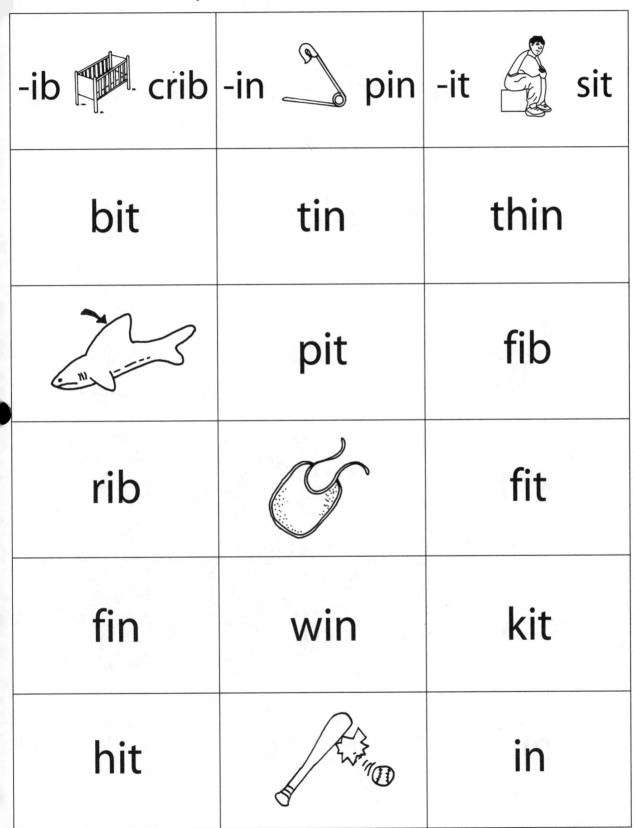

-ib 🛏 crib	-in 🖇 pin	-it 🧍 sit
bit	tin	thin
🦈	pit	fib
rib	🧷	fit
fin	win	kit
hit	⚾	in

SORT 50   Word Family: *id, ick, ill*

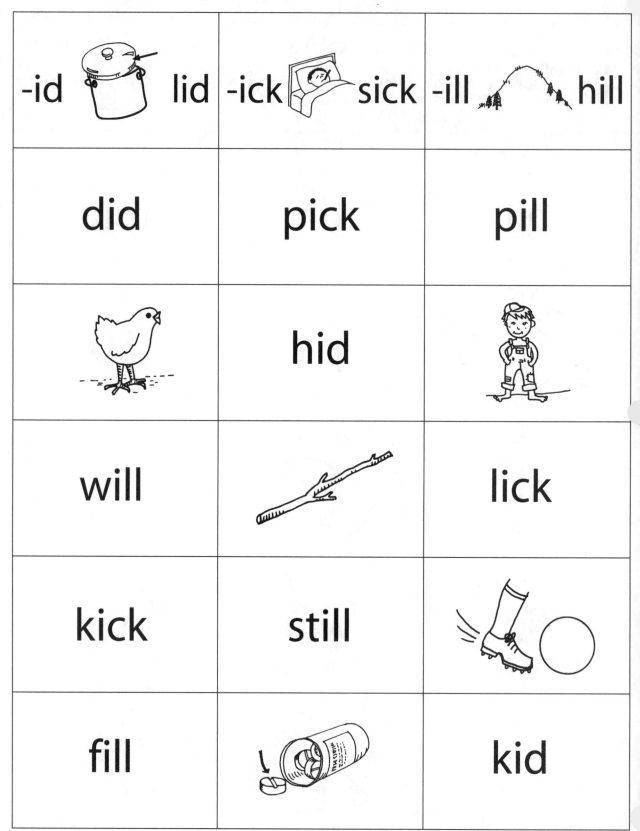

SORT 51   Word Family: *ut, ug*

-ut (nut) nut	-ug (bug) bug	
dug	rug	gut
	shut	hut
but		mug
hug	tug	
cut		snug

SORT 52   Word Family: *ub, um*

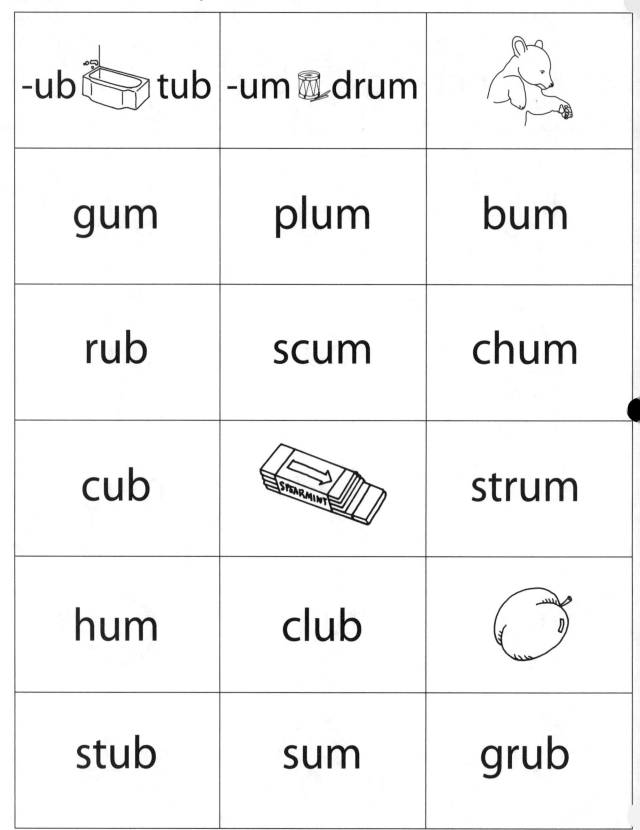

-ub 🛁 tub	-um 🥁 drum	
gum	plum	bum
rub	scum	chum
cub	SPEARMINT	strum
hum	club	
stub	sum	grub

SORT 53   Word Family: *ud, up, un*

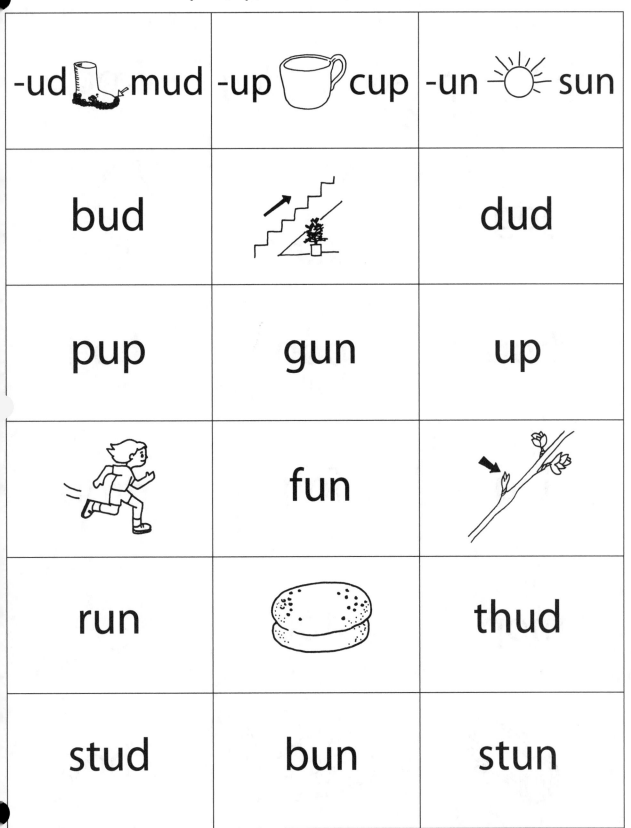

-ud mud	-up cup	-un sun
bud		dud
pup	gun	up
	fun	
run		thud
stud	bun	stun

SORT 54   Word Family: *op, og*

-op 🪀 top	-og 🐕 dog	frog
jog		
hop	pop	hog
log	fog	drop
mop	stop	
		chop

SORT 55   Word Family: *ot, ob*

-ot [pot image] pot	-ob [knob image] knob	bob
mob	got	blob
cot	rob	spot
[knot image]	sob	glob
job	not	[cot image]
cob	lot	hot

SORT 56   Word Family: *od, ock, oss*

-od rod	-ock rock	-oss toss
moss	cross	plod
	clod	
boss	loss	sod
nod	lock	shock
clock		pod

SORT 57   Word Family: *et, en*

-et net	-en hen	(pen)
ten	jet	wet
men	when	met
bet	get	den
pen	then	(jet)
yet	10	let

SORT 58   Word Family: *ed, eg, ell*

-ed bed	-eg leg	-ell bell
	peg	sped
sell	bled	keg
wed	sled	red
beg		
led	tell	shed

Spell Check 7   Assessments of Same-Vowel Word Families

Name _____

1	2	3
hat hot had	mat map mad	big bib bob
4	5	6
pin fan fin	ship lip shop	lad sad had
7	8	9
cab cat nab	hit hill him	dam had ham
10	11	12
dig rug dip	man cap can	sun fit sit
13	14	15
kid lid dad	bat bag rag	pick kick rug

Spell Check 8   Assessments of Same-Vowel Word Families

Name _____

1 hut nut but	2 dot hog dog	3 rod rock pod
4 man mud mush	5 cot cob hot	6 run hug rug
7 tub tug mug	8 sun sock rock	9 men hen ten
10 gum hum got	11 sot sob cob	12 bus bun bug
13 hop mop mad	14 can up cup	15 let leg peg

Unit IX   Mixed-Vowel Word Families

NOTES FOR THE TEACHER

In these word sorts, different vowels will be compared in word families to focus students' attention on the vowel sound. Students continue to practice blending skills as they mix and match onsets (including blends and digraphs) and rimes to figure out words. This reinforces the use of analogy as a decoding strategy. Students will:

- Continue to learn the meaning of words that are useful in their speaking and reading vocabularies
- Sort words by rhyming sound and rime patterns
- Isolate, identify, and blend the onsets and rimes in word families
- Read and spell the words in these sorts

These sorts can be used with middle letter name spellers who are using but confusing short medial vowels and representing consonant blends and digraphs in their spelling. Typically these children are in early to middle first grade and are beginning readers who are acquiring sight words at a good rate. Many English learners who arrive at a later age to schooling in English will be at this stage in later grades as well. Because these sorts use words rather than pictures, it is important that students already know many of the words in each sort such as *cat* and *hat* in the *at* family or *hot* and *pot* in the *ot* family. It is also important that students always say the word aloud as they are sorting it, and that they continue to check that they understand what the word means. Spell Check 9 on page 131 can be used to assess students' proficiency on word families.

These five sorts use word families to contrast vowels. Most students will benefit from spending about a week with each of these sorts because there are more words in each sort and many will not be recognized immediately without repeated practice. We begin with some easier contrasts and end with more difficult distinctions Spanish speakers will need to make, such as the difference between the short *e* and the short *i* word families. There are many more possibilities for word family sorts that are systematically outlined in the appendix of *WTW EL*, so if students need extra practice, look there for additional ideas.

Follow the same standard weekly routines listed for same-vowel word families on pages 95–97, but consider the following additional routines.

1. *Word Study Notebooks.* This is a good time to introduce word study notebooks described in Chapters 5 and 6 of *WTW EL*. Students can list the words from the sort, illustrate some of the words, and write words in sentences. They can also add more words that come from word hunts or are introduced in *build, blend, and extend* lessons.

2. *Blind Sorts or No-Peeking Sorts.* This is a good time to introduce students to blind sorts or no-peeking sorts because they will find it easy to sort visually by the rime pattern. Model this activity first with the group and then let students work with partners under your supervision. After the headers are laid out, students read a word aloud to their partner without showing it. The partner student indicates the

category based on its sound, and points to the header. The word is then laid down immediately to check for accuracy. Students can also do a blind writing sort. As their partner calls a word without showing it, they must write it under the correct header. Be aware, however, that blind sorts can be challenging for students who are learning English. For many learners, seeing the visual of the word can help them conceptualize its pronunciation. So, aim for just the right balance of challenge and support. If students become frustrated, provide visual clues. If they are picking up on the sounds easily, try having them rely more on their ear and memory.

Literature Connection

Make connections to your read-aloud and read-along activities in class by featuring books that include a variety of short-vowel word families such as the following:

Baker, K. *Big fat hen.* (1994). New York: Harcourt, Brace & Company.
Bergman, M. (2005). *Snip snap! What's that?* New York: HarperCollins.
Hillard, S. (2005). *One big hug.* Los Angeles, CA: Mamoo House.
Pinkney, J. (2006). *The little red hen.* New York: Dial Books for Young Readers.
Schwartz, C. R., & Klein, T. (2006). *Hop! Plop!* New York: Walker & Company.
Seuss, D. (1963). *Hop on pop.* New York: Random House.

Demonstrate, Sort, Check, and Reflect

(See page 126.) Prepare a set of pictures and words to use for teacher-directed modeling, such as for Sort 59: *ap/ip/op.*

1. Introduce the words with a **visual sort;** that is, sort first and read the words second. Introduce the labeled pictures as headers, in this case *cap, lip,* and *top.* Explain that the students need to find more words for each word family. Model a word like *map.* Place it under *cap* and then read the header and the word you are placing, saying: Map, cap, *these words go in the same family because they rhyme.* Model several other words, and each time **sort the word first and then read** all of the words from the header down. Allow students to find a visual match rather than trying to read each word ahead of time—they will be more successful at blending if they can use the header as a key word. As each word is sorted, have the students join in as you read them from top to bottom.
2. After sorting all the words, ask the students how the words in each column are alike. Children should note that they rhyme, they are in the same family, and they end in the same two letters.
3. Discuss the meanings of the words, especially those like *tip* or *top* that mean more than one thing. Your completed sort should resemble Sort 59. (See page 123.)
4. Remove the words under each header and let the students repeat the sort together. Again, read all the words down from the top after sorting to check and encourage students to use the header and the growing list of words to support their reading of unfamiliar words. This is important because students are not likely to know how to read all the words in the family without some practice. Once more ask how the words are alike, and whether they can remember what the different words mean.

Sort 59   Word Families: *ap, ip, op*

-ap cap	-ip -lip	-op top
tap	tip	mop
map	dip	hop
snap	sip	shop
rap	hip	stop
lap	zip	drop
gap	rip	pop
clap		chop
nap		

Extend

Give students a copy of the sort to cut apart and use several times on their own. Have them take the sort home to practice with their families. Select from the list of standard weekly routines, including blind sorts or no-peeking sorts.

Completed sorts for the other sorts in this chapter should resemble the following charts.

Sort 60 Word Families: *at, et, ot*

-*at* (hat) hat		-*et* (net) net		-*ot* (pot) pot
cat	mat	let	met	hot
fat	at	bet	get	got
sat	rat	set		not
bat	flat	yet		lot
that		pet		dot

Sort 61 Word Families: *ag, ig, ug*

-*ag* (tag) tag		-*ig* (pig) pig	-*ug* (bug) bug	
wag	bag	dig	dug	snug
sag	drag	big	rug	plug
rag		rig	mug	drug
flag		wig	tug	slug
brag		twig	hug	

Sort 62 Word Families: *ad, ed, id*

-*ad* (pad) pad	-*ed* (bed) bed		-*id* (kid) kid	
dad	fed	sled	skid	hid
mad	led	fled	lid	slid
sad	red		rid	
had	wed		bid	
bad	sped		did	
glad	shed			

Sort 63 Word Families: *an, en, in, un*

-*an* (man) man		-*en* (hen) hen	-*in* (pin) pin	-*un* (sun) sun
van	plan	pen	win	bun
can	than	ten	chin	fun
fan		when	spin	run
tan		men	fin	spun
ran			grin	

SPELL CHECK 9   ASSESSMENT OF MIXED-VOWEL WORD FAMILIES

Mixed-vowel word families are assessed with Spell Check 9 on page 131. This assessment is designed for use as a pretest and/or posttest. To administer the assessment, name each picture and ask students to spell the word that goes with the picture. Students will need you to tell them the names of the words because they may not know the vocabulary independently. Students should be able to spell the entire word correctly at this point!

1. map
2. bag
3. pet
4. wig
5. sad
6. men
7. mop
8. cat
9. bug
10. bed
11. lip
12. chin
13. cot
14. pin
15. kid

SORT 59   Word Families: *ap*, *ip*, *op*

-ap 🧢 cap	-ip 👄 lip	-op 🔺 top
tip	tap	pop
zip	nap	map
hop	sip	mop
snap	rip	stop
gap	dip	rap
shop	lap	drop
clap	chop	hip

SORT 60   Word Families: *at, et, ot*

-at hat	-et net	-ot pot
bet	not	bat
at	set	let
hot	got	cat
fat	met	sat
get	mat	flat
pet	lot	dot
rat	yet	that

SORT 61   Word Families: *ag, ig, ug*

-ag tag	-ig pig	-ug bug
wig	mug	bag
dig	rug	flag
big	hug	rag
slug	drug	drag
plug	twig	dug
rig	tug	sag
snug	brag	wag

SORT 62   Word Families: *ad, ed, id*

-ad pad	-ed bed	-id kid
fed	bad	did
hid	shed	dad
led	had	slid
lid	red	mad
wed	skid	sad
sped	bid	sled
glad	rid	fled

SORT 63   Word Families: *an, en, in, un*

-an man	-en hen	-in pin
-un sun	ran	when
win	than	van
ten	can	run
chin	plan	fun
men	bun	fan
spin	fin	tan
grin	spun	pen

Spell Check 9   Assessment of Mixed-Vowel Word Families

Name _____

Unit X   Ending Sounds

NOTES FOR THE TEACHER

These picture sorts provide explicit opportunities for your students to focus in on ending consonant sounds that are sometimes problematic for Spanish speakers. Each sort features two sounds that are close in articulation to each other, and may be confused by English learners. For example, because the letters *g* and *ck* are pronounced similarly, and words do not end with these sounds in the Spanish writing system, students may have a hard time distinguishing these sounds at the ends of words. It is only with practice and support that students will come to recognize the distinctness of these ending sounds. Remember to be positive and playful as students work with these sounds. Help them to notice the articulatory features of these pairs of sounds. For instance, the /g/ sound has more vibration in the throat, whereas the /k/ is not voiced. The difference between /m/ and /n/ is that the /m/ is made by closing the mouth with the lips, whereas the /n/ is made by closing the mouth with the tongue, and so forth.

You will not necessarily work through each of these sorts with all of your students. Rather, they are provided in case you need to help students who have shown some confusion with these ending sounds in their writing, or in the sorts of the previous chapters. Spell Check 10 on page 141 may also be used as a preassessment guide in choosing the sorts most appropriate to your students' needs.

Standard Weekly Routines for Use with Sorts 64–67

Follow the standard weekly routines noted on pages 95–97. You will use more of these activities depending on the amount of practice and reinforcement students need with the material.

Literature Connection

Help students distinguish difficult ending sounds by listening to, discussing, and chanting along with books that feature words with these sounds. A beginning list is as follows:

Alborough, J. (2005). *Duck in the truck.* La Jolla, CA: Kane Miller Book Publishers.
Ginsburg, M. (1988). *The chick and the duckling.* New York: Aladdin.
Heiligman, D. (2005). *Fun dog, sun dog.* Tarrytown, NY: Marshall Cavendish Corporation.
Schindel, J. (2003). *What did they see?* New York: Henry Holt.
Seuss, D. (1961). *Ten apples up on top.* New York: Random House.
Slobodinka, E. (1987). *Caps for sale.* New York: Harper Trophy. Spanish edition available from Tandem Library.

Demonstrate, Sort, Check, and Reflect

(See page 137.)

1. Prepare a set of pictures to use for teacher-directed modeling. Use the letter/picture cards as headers and display the pictures randomly with the picture side up. Learn the vocabulary of the pictures, as described in the standard weekly routines on pages 95–97. Place the two header cards on the table and make sure that students know their names. For example, *Here is a picture of a bed next to the letter -d and the word bed, a picture of a net next to the letter -t and the word net. In this sort we will be listening to the sound that we hear at the end of a word, not at the beginning. That's why there is a line before the letter, to show it is at the end. Look at the words bed and net. They end with /d/ and /t/. Sometimes those sounds are a little hard to tell apart. We will look for other things that end like bed and net.*

2. Begin a **sound sort** by modeling one word into each column as you explain what you are doing: *Here is a picture of a kid. Kid ends with the /d/ sound made by the letter d. Let's practice saying "kid." Can you feel how the /d/ sounds at the end of the word? Kid sounds like bed at the end, so I will put it under the picture of the bed. This is a picture of a pot. Pot has a /t/ at the end, po-t. I will put it under the picture of the net.* Practice making the ending sounds together, then say, *Now let's sort the rest of these pictures together.* Continue with the children's help to sort all of the pictures. Let mistakes go for now.

3. When all the pictures have been sorted, read each picture in the columns and check for any that need to be changed: *Do all of these sound alike at the end? Do we need to move any?*

4. Repeat the sort with the group again. Keep the letter cards as headers. You may want to mix up the words and turn them face down in a deck this time and let children take turns drawing a card and sorting it in the correct column. You can also simply pass out the pictures and have the children take turns sorting them. After sorting, model how to check by naming the words in each column and then talk about how the words in each column are alike.

5. Give each student a copy of the sort for individual practice. Assign them the task of cutting out the pictures and then sorting on their own in the same way they did in the group. On subsequent days students should repeat the sorting activity several times. Involve the students in the other standard weekly routines described in this book and in *WTW EL* for the letter name–alphabetic stage.

6. Informally assess students on the ending sounds under study throughout the week. Observe students' accuracy and fluency in sorting, and their knowledge of the English vocabulary. At the end of the week, call out four of the words you have been working with, and ask students to write the letter that they hear at the beginning and the end on a small whiteboard or notepaper.

Extend

Have students play a guessing game with a partner. One person thinks of a simple word such as *man*, and says all of the word except its ending sound. The partner must try different ending sounds until he or she guesses the word. Students trade off thinking of words and trying to fool their partner.

Completed sorts should resemble the following charts. Words in parentheses represent pictures.

Sort 64 Ending Sounds: /-d/, /-t/

-d (bed) bed		-t (net) net	
did	dad	(hat)	bat
(rod)	(lid)	pot	(mat)
bad	mad	mat	sat
kid	slid	jet	(cat)

Sort 65 Ending Sounds: /-g/, /-ck/

-g (hug) hug		-ck (rock) rock	
(dog)	(pig)	(block)	sick
rug	wig	chick	(chick)
leg		sack	brick
(rug)		(sock)	stick
bug		pick	

Sort 66 Ending Sounds: /-b/, /-p/

-b (bib) bib		-p (hop) hop	
(crab)	club	(map)	stop
(web)	cab	mop	cup
tub	cub	(top)	
crib	ship	nap	
web		rip	

Sort 67 Ending Sounds: /-m/, /-n/

-m (gum) gum		-n (fan) fan	
mom	swim	ten	(bun)
dam	(swim)	pin	grin
ham	plum	sun	
drum	stem	can	
(drum)		(man)	

SPELL CHECK 10   ASSESSMENT OF ENDING SOUNDS

Ending sounds are assessed with Spell Check 10 on page 141. This assessment is designed for use as a pretest and/or posttest. To administer the assessment, name each picture and have students circle the correct spelling of the word. Be sure to clearly say the ending sound of each word, and look directly at students while dictating the words. If students identify the sounds correctly, they probably do not need more focused work in this area. If they continue to have difficulty distinguishing these sounds or representing them in their writing, more in-depth work is needed. The pictures in Spell Check 10 are as follows:

1. hug	2. web	3. drum
4. ten	5. sock	6. chin
7. lid	8. map	9. jet
10. swim	11. hot	12. mop

SORT 64   Ending Sounds: /-d/, /-t/

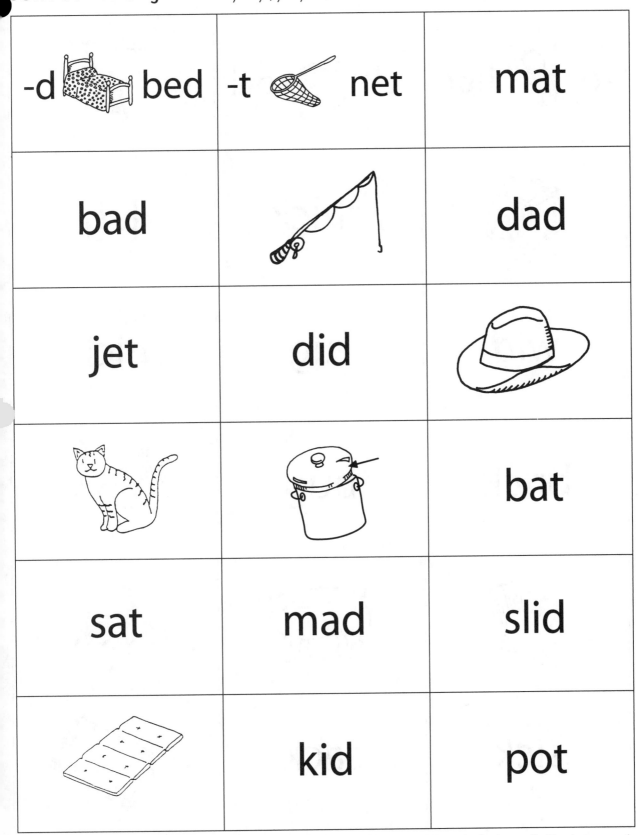

-d [bed] bed	-t [net] net	mat
bad	[fishing pole]	dad
jet	did	[hat]
[cat]	[pot]	bat
sat	mad	slid
[mat]	kid	pot

SORT 65   Ending Sounds: /-g/, /-ck/

-g hug	-ck rock	
	chick	leg
wig	rug	pick
brick	bug	
		stick
sick	sack	

SORT 66   Ending Sounds: /-b/, /-p/

-b 🖱 bib	-p 🏃 hop	club
🗺	tub	cup
nap	web	🦀
cab	🌀	cub
mop	ship	crib
stop	🕸	rip

SORT 67   Ending Sounds: /-m/, /-n/

-m gum	-n fan	mom
ham	dam	stem
	pin	
sun	drum	grin
can		swim
	plum	ten

Spell Check 10   Assessment of Ending Sounds

Name _____

1 hug huck	2 wep web	3 drun drum
4 ten tem	5 sog sock	6 chim chin
7 lid lit	8 mab map	9 jed jet
10 swin swim	11 hod hot	12 mob mop

Unit XI   Short Vowels in CVC Words

NOTES FOR THE TEACHER

In these word sorts, different short vowels will be compared without the support of word families. Instead students will learn to recognize the CVC pattern (consonant-vowel-consonant as in *bat* or *brat* or *blast*) in connection with the short-vowel sounds. In the next stage, within word patterns, this CVC pattern will be compared with long-vowel patterns. Students will:

- Segment all the sounds in a CVC word and identify the short-vowel sound
- Spell unit words with short vowels, blends, and digraphs correctly

These sorts can be used with students in the late letter name stage who are using but confusing medial vowels, consonant blends, and digraphs. On a spelling inventory they should spell most blends and digraphs correctly and spell a few short vowels correctly as well. Their confusions often relate to sounds that are distinct in English, or close contrasts such as /sh/ and /ch/. Students at this stage are often at a middle to late first-grade level, but students with limited formal schooling may be at this stage into the later elementary grades as well. Students should know how to read many CVC words already from their reading. These sorts may be used for review of short vowels at the beginning of second grade or beyond with any students who need work on short vowels, blends, or digraphs. Spell Check 11 on page 153 can be used as a pretest or posttest for mastery.

It is important that students already know most of the words in each sort, and many of the words studied earlier in word families will reappear here. The CVC words included here have been selected because they are the most common and useful in beginning reading materials and oral language. It continues to be important that students understand the meaning of all of the words they sort. Otherwise, word study becomes a rote task that does not seem authentic. If students cannot recognize the words, or do not easily learn their meanings, set them aside for the time being. If this is the case, feel free to substitute other words into the sort that are more familiar. Expect that students who are familiar with sorting by families may be a little confused at first when they are asked to focus just on the vowel. Modeling the sort several times will help them learn where to direct their attention.

There are five sorts that contrast short vowels. The contrasts move from fairly easy (short *a* and short *o*) to extremely difficult (short *e* and short *i*). Students who only need a quick review can move through the sorts at a brisk pace—perhaps doing a new sort every 3 to 4 days. Because the sounds of short vowels are hard to distinguish for Spanish speakers, however, most students will need a slower, more in-depth pace. Do not expect students to necessarily master the slight distinctions between short-vowel sounds, such as the difference between *pin* and *pen*. Be supportive and provide lots of practice, but know that students will refine their knowledge as they read more and increase their sight word vocabulary. The next section (Sorts 73 to 77) also provides reinforcement of short vowels in CVC words with consonant blends and digraphs. If students are having difficulty, you might want to create additional sorts by writing words from the appendix of *WTW EL* on the blank template at the end of this book.

Standard Weekly Routines for Word Sorts 68–72

1. *Repeated Work with the Words.*   Students should work with the featured sorts several times after the sort has been modeled and discussed in the group. If you have not yet done so, this is a good place to establish homework routines. Have students take their sort home and demonstrate it for their families. Have them repeat the sort, always saying the words aloud, until it becomes fluent and automatic.

2. *Writing Sorts and Word Study Notebooks.*   Students should record their word sorts by writing them into columns under the key words established in the group sort. Students may be asked to select some words to illustrate or to use some of them (not *all* of them) in sentences to demonstrate the meaning of the words.

3. *Blind or No-peeking Sorts and Writing Sorts.*   Doing these with a partner (described in Chapter 3 of *WTW EL*) is especially important so that students focus on sound as well as what they see in the printed word.

4. *Word Building, Blending, and Extending.*   Activities may now isolate the vowel to explore the CVC pattern in which there are three units to blend or spell as in *g-u-m*.

5. *Word Hunts.*   Look for words in daily reading materials that mirror the featured vowel sounds. Word hunts can extend children's understanding when they include longer words such as *mitten* or *tablet* that have short-vowel sounds in one or more syllables.

6. *Games and Other Activities.*   Continue to play games and use manipulatives to practice the short-vowel words. Many games are described in Chapters 5 and 6 of *WTW EL.* Games provide a fun way to engage with the tricky sounds of the short vowels in a less stressful environment.

7. *Assessment.*   A weekly spelling test may become part of your routine by the late letter name stage. You may also want to select additional CVC words for testing to see how well students can transfer their mastery of features.

Literature Connection

The following picture books have reoccurring words that use short-vowels. Students will enjoy finding these words in the stories you are reading, and comparing words that have different short-vowel sounds. You will find many opportunities for identifying and discussing these words in your book-sharing activities with these and other books in your collection.

Clements, A. (1997). *Big Al.* New York: Aladdin Paperbacks.

Cousins, L. (2000). *Maisy drives the bus.* Cambridge, MA: Candlewick Press.

Cronin, D. (2003). *Click, clack, moo: Cows that type.* New York: Simon & Schuster.

Grant, J. (2006). *Cat and fish go to see.* Vancouver, BC: Simply Read Books.

Pomerantz, C. (1974). *The piggy in the puddle.* New York: Simon & Schuster.

Wood, D. (2001). *What moms can't do.* New York: Scholastic.

Demonstrate, Sort, Check, and Reflect

(See page 148.)

1. Prepare a set of words to use for teacher-directed modeling. This sort might be used in connection with the short-vowel *a* and *o* in Sort 68. You will first sort the pictures

to practice hearing the short-vowel sounds, then turn to the word sort. Later in the week, students can glue down the picture sort and label the words.

2. Display the words and begin by asking the students to read over them to see if there are any they do not know or understand. Help them read and discuss the meaning of any that are unfamiliar.

3. Pull out the labeled headers *man* and *tub*. Model a word such as *ham*. Place it under *man*, reading the header and the word under it saying, *Haaaam, maaaan—these words have the same vowel sound in the middle.* (You can isolate the vowel by covering the letters in the word as you say *man, an, a.*) Model several other words by reading the word and comparing it to the two headers.

4. Begin calling on students to decide where to place the other words. After sorting all the words, read them from the top and ask students how the words in each column are alike. Introduce the term "short vowel" by saying something like, *These words have the short -a sound and these have the short -u sound.* Children should note that each column has the same vowel spelling and sound. Point out that these words all have a similar pattern called CVC that stands for consonant, vowel, consonant. Sort 68 should resemble the following:

Sort 68   Short *a* and *u* Vowels

ă		ŭ	
ham	am	mud	bus
bad	pan	run	club
mad	rag	gum	fun
bat	chat	bug	but
wax	ran	cut	up
tap	than		

5. Because these words can simply be sorted visually by looking at the letters in the word, the second sort should be done by **sound**. Keep the same headers, but this time, the teacher should say the word without showing it. Students take turns identifying where the word will go and can check as soon as the word is placed in the column.

Extend

Students should get their own words for sorts and engage in the standard weekly routines suggested on page 144. We especially encourage you to ensure that your students are getting plenty of oral practice with the words, by having students work with a peer partner or a family member in a blind sort, and in always saying the sort words aloud.

Sort 69 Short *e* and *u* Vowels

ĕ (web)		ŭ (cup)	
pet	men	but	us
get	ten	cut	up
fed	jet	gum	dug
yet	let	run	rug
red	wet	bun	
leg	them	mug	

Sort 70 Short *i* and *a* Vowels

ĭ (pig)		ă (man)	
him	six	at	that
his	big	lad	than
will	did	bag	trap
if	sit	pal	ran
with	hit	lap	
is	chip	had	

Sort 71 Short *o* and *u* Vowels

ŏ (mop)		ŭ (cup)	
mop	box	nut	but
log	got	bud	plum
job	spot	pup	such
fox	chop	drum	rub
mom	top	thud	
stop	not	much	

Sort 72 Short *e* and *i* Vowels

ĕ (web)		ĭ (pig)	
get	wet	big	hit
leg	men	him	will
beg	wed	sit	rip
set	yet	fix	mix
jet	yes	his	
when	then	did	

SPELL CHECK 11 ASSESSMENT FOR SHORT VOWELS

A form is provided at the end of the short-vowel sorts for students to use. Call the following words aloud for students to spell. Evaluate each word for correct spelling of the short vowel as well as for the beginning and ending sounds. The pictures in this spell check are:

1. bat	**2.** log	**3.** hen
4. rug	**5.** fin	**6.** sob
7. leg	**8.** bag	**9.** rip
10. six	**11.** bun	**12.** plum

SORT 68   Short *a* and *u* Vowels

ă	ŭ	mad
run	bug	tap
bus	pan	mud
rag	gum	ham
cut	bad	club
bat	wax	fun
am	but	chat
ran	up	than

SORT 69   Short *e* and *u* Vowels

ĕ	ŭ	fed
but	run	leg
bun	ten	pet
cut	gum	yet
get	mug	red
them	men	us
up	jet	let
dug	wet	rug

SORT 70   Short *i* and *a* Vowels

ĭ	ă	at
if	lap	is
six	bag	him
lad	with	pal
will	his	that
big	had	did
than	sit	trap
hit	chip	ran

SORT 71   Short *o* and *u* Vowels

ŏ	ŭ	job
pup	mom	much
plum	got	mop
bud	log	drum
thud	fox	but
stop	spot	box
nut	chop	such
top	rub	not

SORT 72   Short *e* and *i* Vowels

ĕ	ĭ	beg
rip	jet	big
mix	men	set
him	wed	then
his	yet	hit
yes	wet	sit
fix	get	leg
did	when	will

Spell Check 11   Assessment for Short Vowels

Name _____

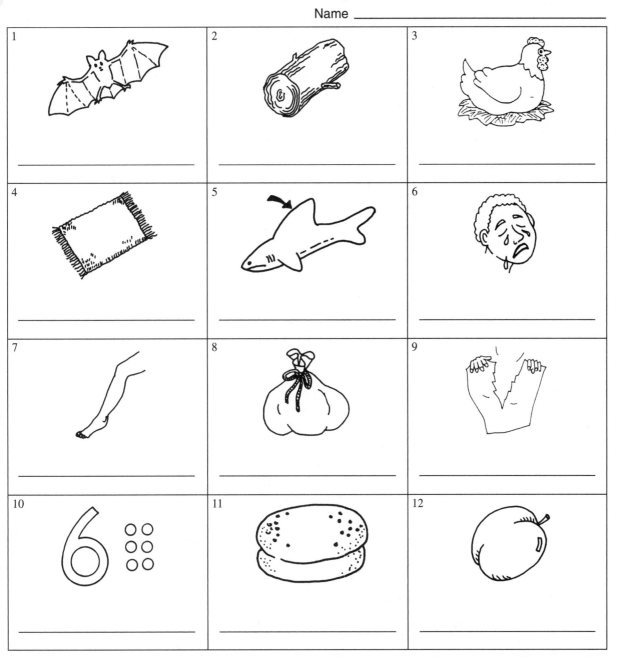

Unit XII   Beginning Digraphs and Blends in CVC Words

NOTES FOR THE TEACHER

In this unit we continue our work with the CVC pattern, this time in words with beginning digraphs or blends. We are systematically increasing the difficulty of short-vowel words to help students build a strong foundation in the CVC pattern. The final sorts (78 to 81) take the pattern one step further by examining complex CVC words that have ending digraphs and blends, including preconsonantal nasals.

Explain to students that although the words here may begin with two consonants, such as *ch* in *chip* or *st* in *step*, they should look at the blend or digraph as one unit—the first C of the CVC pattern. Having two consonants at the beginning of a word does not affect the sound of the short vowel. If you notice students becoming confused about the vowel sounds with these words, take a step back with simpler words, and help them gain security with what they already know.

Also, remember that certain sounds can be quite challenging for Spanish speakers, such as the difference between the sound of /ch/ and /sh/, or /th/ with /d/ or /t/. If needed, go back to picture Sorts 19 to 34 to reinforce the sound distinctions students have already practiced.

Standard Weekly Routines for use with Initial Digraphs and Blends in Sorts 73–77

Continue to use the routines outlined for word sorts on page 144. Some unusual words appear in these sorts, such as *chum* or *blip*. Take the time to discuss the meanings of these words and use them in context. Insist that students say their sorting words aloud when they do them with you or on their own. In addition to keeping track of sorting words in their word study notebooks, students may also want to keep an illustrated dictionary in which they note words that begin with blends or digraphs.

Literature Connection

Following are picture books that feature words with beginning consonant digraphs and blends. Students will enjoy hearing and reading these words in the stories, and chanting patterns such as, "trip, trap, trip, trap." You will find many opportunities for identifying and discussing blends and digraphs in your book-sharing activities with these and other books in your collection.

Derby, S. (1999). *My steps.* New York: Lee and Low Books. Spanish edition also available.

Galdone, P. (1981). *The three billy goats Gruff.* New York: Clarion Books.

Harrington, J. N. (2007). *The chicken-chasing queen of Lamar County.* New York: Farrar, Straus & Giroux.

Lies, B. (2006). *Bats at the beach.* Boston: Houghton Mifflin.

Luján, J. (2006). *Sky blue accident/Accidente celeste.* Berkeley, CA: Groundwood Books.

O'Connor, J. (2007). *Ready, set, skip.* New York: Viking.

Weeks, S. (2000). *Drip, drop (An I can read book).* New York: HarperTrophy.

Demonstrate, Sort, Check, and Reflect

(See page 161.)

1. Prepare a set of words to use for teacher-directed modeling. Use the letter/picture cards as headers and display the words randomly with word side up. Learn the vocabulary of the pictures, as described in the standard weekly routines on page 144. Place the header cards on the table and make sure that students know their names. For example, *Here is a picture of a thumb next to the letters* th, *a chair next to the letters* ch, *and a hen next to the letter* h. Ch *is two letters put together to make one sound* /ch/ *and* th, *the sound* /th/. *We will be sorting CVC words, and some of them begin with two letters that make one sound.*

2. Begin with an **open sort,** asking the students for their ideas about categories: *Who has an idea about how to sort these words? Is there another way?* These words should be sorted by the short-vowel sound but also by the beginning digraph; both of these should be modeled in the group. Reading these words may be challenging because of the initial digraph. Help students look at these words as onsets (in this case a digraph) and rimes they have seen in previous sorts (*-at, -ip, -in,* etc.). They still fit the CVC pattern because a digraph is a consonant unit. Note that *th* has two slightly different sounds in these words. In *then, them, this,* and *that* the sound is voiced, and in *thin* and *thud* the sound is unvoiced. This difference is felt in the vocal cords rather than in the mouth and is often completely overlooked by speakers of English. Digraph Sort 73 will look something like the one shown here.

Sort 73 Beginning Digraphs: *ch, th, h*

ch	th	h
chop	this	hat
chin	thin	hut
check	them	hid
chip	then	hem
chap	that	ham
chug	thud	has
chat		hog
chum		

3. When all the pictures have been sorted, read each picture in the columns and check for any that need to be changed: *Do all of these sound alike at the beginning? Do we need to move any?*

4. Repeat the sort with the group again. Keep the letter cards as headers. You may want to mix up the words and turn them face down in a deck this time and let children take turns drawing a card and sorting it in the correct column. You can also simply pass out the pictures and have the children take turns sorting them. After sorting, model how to check by naming the words in each column and then talk about how the words in each column are alike.

5. Next, ask students if there is another way to sort the words. If necessary, remind them of the short-vowel sorts they have been doing, and suggest that they look at the short vowels in the words. You will not want to use the same header cards for this sort, as these headers are based on the beginning sound. Help students isolate the vowel sound in each word as you did in Sorts 68 to 72. Your completed vowel sort should resemble the following:

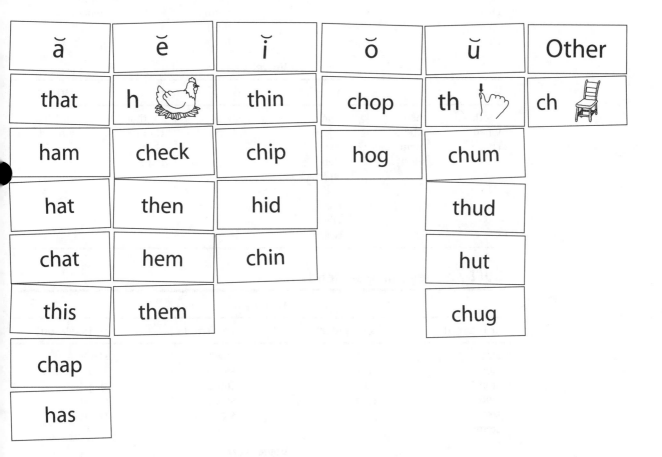

ă	ĕ	ĭ	ŏ	ŭ	Other
that	h 🐓	thin	chop	th 👆	ch 🪑
ham	check	chip	hog	chum	
hat	then	hid		thud	
chat	hem	chin		hut	
this	them			chug	
chap					
has					

6. Give each student a copy of the sort for individual practice. On subsequent days, students should repeat the sorting activity several times. Involve the students in the other weekly routines described in this book and in *WTW EL* Chapter 5.

7. Informally assess students on CVC words with beginning digraphs and blends throughout the week. Observe students' accuracy and fluency in sorting, and their knowledge of the English vocabulary. At the end of the week, call out four to six words you have been working with, and ask students to write them on a small whiteboard or notepaper.

Extend

If you find that your students have difficulty distinguishing the sounds of the beginning consonant digraphs and blends, you might want to prepare additional sorts that contrast the letters or sounds they are confusing. There are pictures and a template available in *WTW EL* to use for this purpose.

Completed examples for Sort 73 are provided already. The other completed sorts should resemble the following charts. Words in parentheses represent pictures.

Sort 74 Beginning Digraphs: *ch, sh, th, wh*

Digraph sort			
ch (chair)	**sh (ship)**	**th (thumb)**	**wh (whale)**
chop	shop	then	when
chin	shack	this	whip
chat	shut	them	wham
chum	shed	thud	whiz
chip	shin	thin	which

			Vowel sort		
ă	**ě**	**ĭ**	**ŏ**	**ŭ**	**Other**
shack	then	chin	shop	th (thumb)	ch (chair)
wham	when	this	chop	chum	wh (whale)
chat	them	chip		shut	
	shed	shin		thud	
		sh (ship)			
		whip			
		thin			
		whiz			
		which			

Sort 75 Beginning *s*-Blends

Blend sort			
st (stamp)	**sp (spider)**	**sm (smoke)**	**sk (skeleton)**
stab	spill	smell	skit
stuck	spot	smack	skid
stop	spit	smog	skill
stub	span	smug	skin
step		smash	skim
stem			

			Vowel sort		
ă	**ě**	**ĭ**	**ŏ**	**ŭ**	**Other**
stab	step	spill	stop	stuck	sp (spider)
span	stem	spit	spot	stub	sm (smoke)
smack	smell	skit	smog	smug	sk (skeleton)
smash		skid			
st (stamp)		skill			
		skin			
		skim			

Sort 76 Beginning *l*-Blends

Blend sort

bl (block)	fl (flag)	cl (clock)	sl (sled)
black	flop	clap	slam
blab	flip	clip	slap
blast	flesh	cloth	slim
blob	flap	class	slip
blip	flash		
	flat		
	floss		

Vowel sort

ă	ĕ	ĭ	ŏ
fl (flag)	sl (sled)	blip	bl (block)
black	flesh	flip	cl (clock)
blab		clip	blob
blast		slim	flop
flap		slip	floss
flash			cloth
flat			
clap			
class			
slam			
slap			

Sort 77 Beginning *r*-Blends

Blend sort

br (brush)	gr (grass)	fr (frog)	tr (tree)
brush	grim	from	trim
brim	grin	frost	trot
brick	grid	fresh	trust
brat	grip		truck
brag	grab		trash
			trap
			trip

Vowel sort

ă	ĕ	ĭ	ŏ	ŭ	Other
gr (grass)	fresh	brim	fr (frog)	br (brush)	tr (tree)
brat		brick	frost	brush	from
brag		grim	trot	trust	
grab		grin		truck	
trash		grid			
trap		grip			
		trip			
		trim			

SPELL CHECK 12 ASSESSMENT OF BEGINNING CONSONANT DIGRAPHS AND BLENDS

A form is provided at the end of this chapter for student use. Call the following words aloud for students to spell. Evaluate each word for correct spelling of the short vowel as well as for the beginning and ending sounds. The pictures in this spell check are:

1. stop
4. sled
7. chin
10. clap

2. ship
5. frog
8. whip
11. spill

3. chop
6. flag
9. brush
12. block

SORT 73   Beginning Digraphs: *ch, th, h*

ch	th	h
chip	this	hat
chat	hem	chop
thin	ham	hog
chap	thud	hut
chin	that	chum
hid	check	then
has	chug	them

SORT 74   Beginning Digraphs: *ch, sh, th, wh*

ch	sh	th
wh	chip	shop
when	thud	chop
shack	them	shed
which	then	shin
chum	shut	this
chin	wham	whiz
thin	whip	chat

SORT 75   Beginning s-Blends

st	sp	sm
sk	step	spot
skit	stab	spill
stuck	smack	span
smell	stop	skim
smog	spit	skid
stub	smug	skill
smash	stem	skin

SORT 76 Beginning *l*-Blends

bl	fl	cl
sl	flip	black
clap	floss	cloth
blob	slam	flap
slim	flat	blast
flesh	flop	slip
blab	class	slap
blip	flash	clip

SORT 77   Beginning *r*-Blends

br	gr	fr
tr	from	brag
trap	grab	brush
truck	grid	trip
brim	trash	frost
grim	grip	trot
brat	trim	grin
trust	fresh	brick

Spell Check 12   Assessment of Beginning Consonant Digraphs and Blends

Name _____

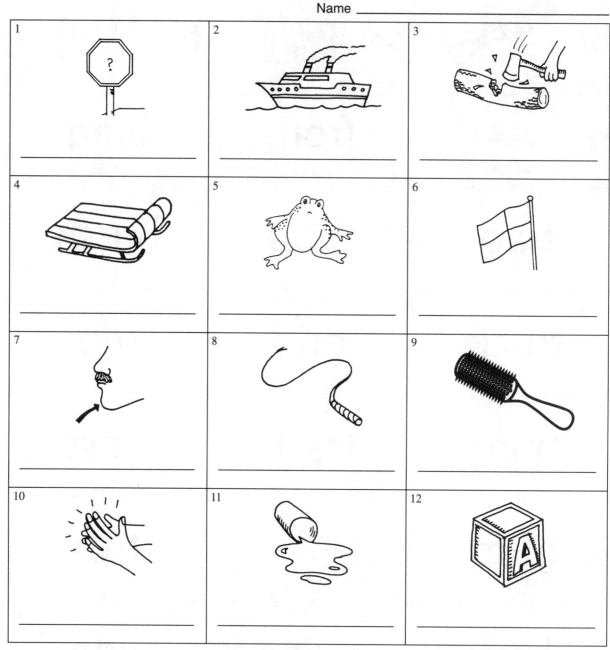

Unit XIII   Ending Digraphs and Blends in CVC Words

NOTES FOR THE TEACHER

In this unit we continue our work with the CVC pattern, this time in words with ending digraphs or blends. We are systematically increasing the difficulty of short-vowel words to help students build a strong foundation in the CVC pattern. As we move to the close of this book we work with students on complex CVC words that have ending digraphs and blends, including preconsonantal nasals. A preconsonantal nasal is a nasal sound, like /m/ or /n/ that precedes another consonant, such as in the words *bump* or *land*. This is one of the most difficult sounds for letter name–alphabetic spellers to perceive, and when students begin to use but confuse it, they are nearly in the within word pattern stage. This process is even more difficult for Spanish speakers, because as mentioned, the Spanish language does not end words with most consonants, and especially not with blend or digraphs.

Explain to students that although the words we are examining may end or begin with two consonants, such as *sh* in *wish* or *st* in *vest*, they should look at the blend or digraph as one unit—the second C of the CVC pattern. Having two consonants at the end of a word does not change the sound of a short-vowel word. If you notice students becoming confused about the vowel sounds as the CVC patterns get more complex, then take a step back with simpler words to help them gain security in what they already know.

Also, remember that certain sounds can be quite challenging for Spanish speakers, such as the difference between the sound of /ch/ and /sh/, or /th/ with /d/ or /t/. If needed, go back to picture Sorts 19 to 34 to reinforce the sound distinctions students have already practiced.

Standard Weekly Routines for Use with Ending Digraphs and Blends in Sorts 78–81

Continue to use the routines outlined for word sorts on page 144. Some less frequent words appear in these sorts, such as *prong* or *spilt*. Take the time to discuss the meanings of these words and use them in context. Insist that students say their sorting words aloud when they do them with you or on their own. In addition to keeping track of sorting words in their word study notebooks, students may also want to keep an illustrated dictionary in which they note words that contain blends or digraphs.

Literature Connection

Following are picture books that feature words with ending consonant digraphs and blends. Students will enjoy hearing and identifying these sounds and spellings in the stories, and being playful with words such as *splish* and *splash*. You will find many opportunities for identifying and discussing ending blends and digraphs in your book-sharing activities with these and other books in your collection.

Bottner, B. (2003). *Pish and Posh* (I Can Read Book 2). New York: Katherine Tegen Books, an imprint of HarperCollins.

Florian, D. (2005). *Zoo's who.* New York: Harcourt Children's Books.

Foley, G. (2007). *Thank you bear.* New York: Viking Juvenile.

Sayre, A. P. (2005). *Ant, ant, ant (an insect chant).* Minocqua, WI: NorthWord Books for Young Readers.

Tankard, J. (2007). *Grumpy bird.* New York: Scholastic Press.

Weeks, S. (1999). *Splish, splash!* (My first I can read). New York: Harper Trophy.

Demonstrate, Sort, Check, and Reflect

(See page 172.)

1. Prepare a set of words to use for teacher-directed modeling. Use the letter / picture cards as headers and display the words randomly with word side up. Learn the vocabulary of the pictures, as described in the standard weekly routines throughout this book. Place the header cards on the table and make sure that students know their names. For example, *Here is a picture of a peach next to the letters -ch, a bath next to the letters -th, and a fish next to the letters -sh. We have worked many times with two letters that either make one sound, or blend together to start or end a word. Now we will be sorting CVC words, and some of them end with two letters that make one sound, or two letters that make a blend.*

2. Begin with an **open sort,** asking the students for their ideas about categories: *Who has an idea about how to sort these words? Is there another way?* These words should be sorted by the short-vowel sound but also by the ending digraph; both of these should be modeled in the group. Reading these words may be challenging because of the digraphs and blends at the beginning or ends of words. Help students look at these words as having a sound unit (in this case a digraph) at the end. They still fit the CVC pattern because a digraph or a blend is a consonant unit. Digraph Sort 78 will look something like the one shown here.

Sort 78 Ending Digraphs: *-ch, -th, -sh*

-ch	-th	-sh
such	bath	slush
clutch	with	wish
crutch	math	smash
rich	fifth	crush
which	cloth	fish
much	broth	stash
	moth	mesh
		cash

3. When all the pictures have been sorted, read each picture in the columns and check for any that need to be changed: *Do all of these sound alike at the end? Do we need to move any?*

4. Repeat the sort with the group again. Keep the letter cards as headers. You may want to mix up the words and turn them face down in a deck this time and let children take turns drawing a card and sorting it in the correct column. You can also simply pass out the pictures and have the children take turns sorting them. After sorting, model how to check by naming the words in each column and then talk about how the words in each column are alike.

5. Next, ask students if there is another way to sort the words. If necessary, remind them of the short-vowel sorts they have been doing, and suggest that they look at the short vowels in the words. You will not want to use the same header cards for this sort, as these headers are based on the ending sound. Help students isolate the vowel sound in each word as you did in Sorts 68 through 77. Your completed vowel sort should look something like the following:

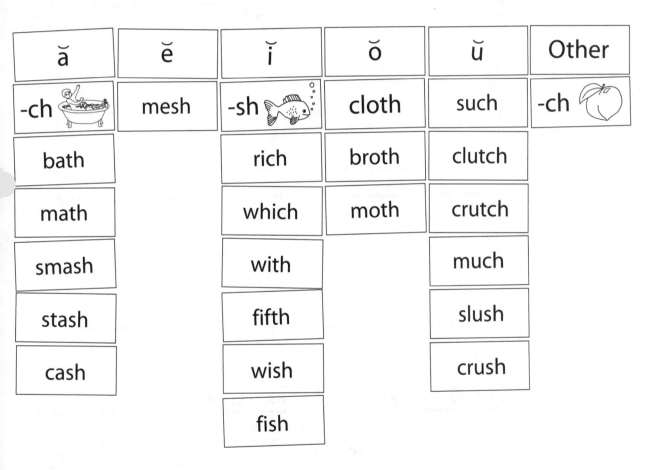

ă	ĕ	ĭ	ŏ	ŭ	Other
-ch	mesh	-sh	cloth	such	-ch
bath		rich	broth	clutch	
math		which	moth	crutch	
smash		with		much	
stash		fifth		slush	
cash		wish		crush	
		fish			

6. Give each student a copy of the sort for individual practice. On subsequent days, students should repeat the sorting activity several times. Involve the students in the other weekly routines described in this book and in *WTW EL* Chapter 5.

7. Informally assess students on CVC words with ending digraphs and blends throughout the week. Observe students' accuracy and fluency in sorting, and their knowledge of the English vocabulary. At the end of the week, call out four to six words you have been working with, and ask students to write them on a small whiteboard or notepaper.

Extend

If you find that your students have difficulty distinguishing the sounds of the ending consonant digraphs and blends, you might want to prepare additional sorts that contrast the letters or sounds they are confusing. There are pictures and a template available in *WTW EL* to use for this purpose. If preconsonantal nasals are too difficult for your students at this point, spend additional time on a range of complex, short-vowel words with beginning and ending blends and digraphs, such as *swift* and *stash*.

Completed examples for Sort 78 are already shown. The other completed sorts should resemble the following charts. Words in parentheses represent pictures.

Sort 79   Ending Blends: *-t, -st, -ft*

Ending sound sort		
-t (cat)	**-st (nest)**	**-ft (gift)**
hit	list	craft
hot	vest	drift
kit	test	theft
not	blast	soft
bet	cost	raft
vet	pest	swift
that	dust	left

Vowel sort				
ă	**ĕ**	**ĭ**	**ŏ**	**ŭ**
-t (cat)	-st (nest)	-ft (gift)	hot	dust
that	bet	hit	not	
blast	vet	kit	cost	
craft	vest	list	soft	
raft	test	drift		
	pest	swift		
	theft			
	left			

Sort 80   Ending Blends: *-mp, -nd, -ng, -nt*

Ending sound sort			
-mp (lamp)	**-nd (hand)**	**-ng (wing)**	**-nt (tent)**
tramp	end	song	dent
limp	stand	hang	lint
	sand	cling	pant
	wind	prong	bent
	pond	king	runt
		sting	chant
		bang	

Vowel sort

ă	ĕ	ĭ	ŏ	ŭ
-mp (lamp)	-nt (tent)	-ng (wing)	pond	runt
-nd (hand)	end	limp	song	
tramp	dent	wind	prong	
stand	bent	cling		
sand		king		
hang		sting		
bang		lint		
pant				
chant				

Sort 81 Ending Blends: *-lp, -lk, -lf, -lt*

Ending sound sort

-lp he<u>lp</u>	-lk mi<u>lk</u>	-lf e<u>lf</u>	-lt be<u>lt</u>
gulp	elk	self	felt
scalp	bulk	golf	melt
kelp		gulf	quilt
yelp			wilt
pulp			spilt
shelf			
silk			

Vowel sort

ă	ĕ	ĭ	ŏ	ŭ
scalp	-lp he<u>lp</u>	-lk milk	golf	gulp
	-lf e<u>lf</u>	silk		pulp
	-lt be<u>lt</u>	quilt		bulk
	kelp	wilt		gulf
	yelp	spilt		
	shelf			
	elk			
	self			
	felt			
	melt			

SPELL CHECK 13   ASSESSMENT OF ENDING CONSONANT DIGRAPHS AND BLENDS

A form is provided at the end of this chapter for students to use. Call the following words aloud for students to spell. Evaluate each word for correct spelling of the short vowel as well as for the beginning and ending sounds. The pictures in this spell check are:

1. bath
2. fish
3. nest
4. shelf
5. quilt
6. gift
7. king
8. hand
9. tent
10. golf
11. plant
12. sting

SORT 78   Ending Digraphs: *-ch, -th, -sh*

-ch	-th	-sh
fish	cloth	crush
rich	smash	clutch
bath	slush	stash
mesh	broth	fifth
much	such	crutch
cash	wish	with
which	math	moth

SORT 79   Ending Blends: -t, -st, -ft

-t	-st	-ft
craft	left	not
list	blast	theft
drift	bet	dust
cost	soft	raft
hit	swift	pest
hot	that	vet
vest	kit	test

SORT 80   Ending Blends: *-mp, -nd, -ng, -nt*

-mp	-nd	-ng
-nt	bang	dent
pond	limp	tramp
hang	sand	runt
king	chant	wind
sting	song	end
lint	prong	pant
stand	cling	bent

SORT 81 Ending Blends: *-lp, -lk, -lf, -lt*

-lp hel<u>p</u>	-lk mi<u>lk</u>	-lf el<u>f</u>
-lt be<u>lt</u>	pulp	shelf
silk	yelp	elk
golf	felt	gulp
scalp	melt	bulk
gulf	quilt	wilt
spilt	self	kelp

Spell Check 13   Assessment of Ending Consonant Digraphs and Blends

Name _____

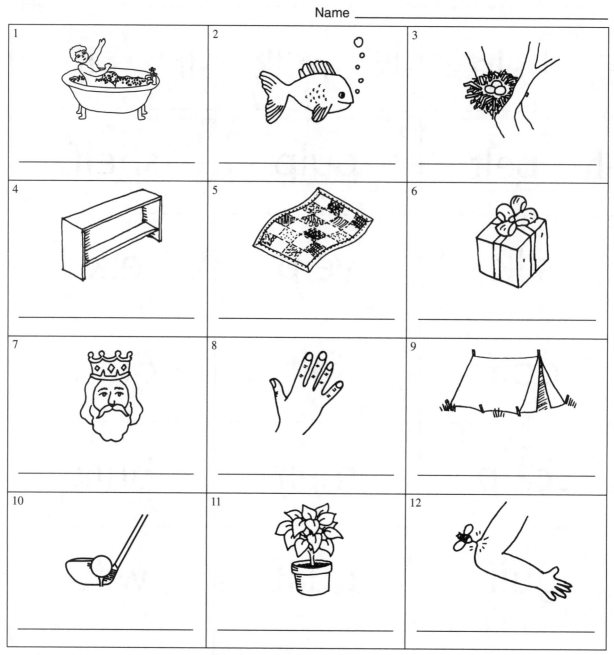

Appendix

Bilingual Picture Alphabet—English/Spanish

Letter Cards for Building, Blending, and Extending
   Word Families
   Digraphs and Blends
   Word Families
   Short Vowels and Final Clusters

Blank Template for Picture Sorts

Blank Template for Word Sorts

Bilingual Picture Alphabet—English/Spanish

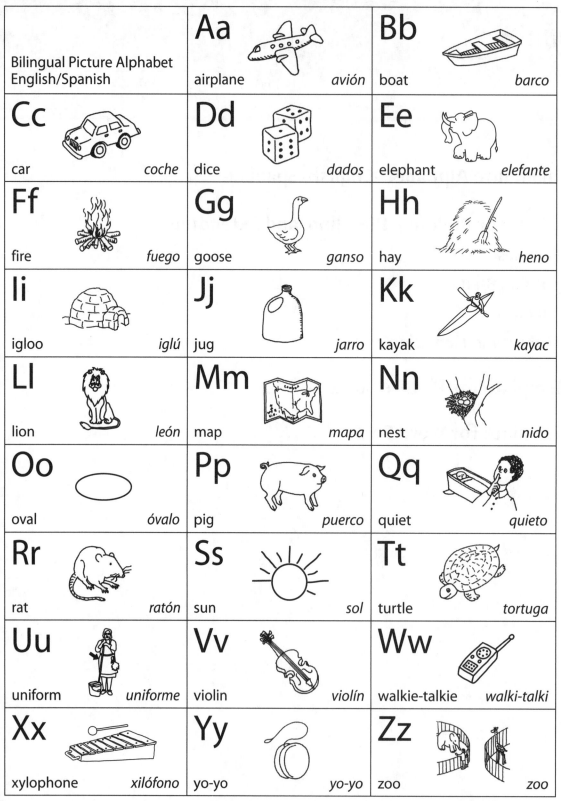

Bilingual Picture Alphabet English/Spanish	Aa airplane *avión*	Bb boat *barco*
Cc car *coche*	Dd dice *dados*	Ee elephant *elefante*
Ff fire *fuego*	Gg goose *ganso*	Hh hay *heno*
Ii igloo *iglú*	Jj jug *jarro*	Kk kayak *kayac*
Ll lion *león*	Mm map *mapa*	Nn nest *nido*
Oo oval *óvalo*	Pp pig *puerco*	Qq quiet *quieto*
Rr rat *ratón*	Ss sun *sol*	Tt turtle *tortuga*
Uu uniform *uniforme*	Vv violin *violín*	Ww walkie-talkie *walki-talki*
Xx xylophone *xilófono*	Yy yo-yo *yo-yo*	Zz zoo *zoo*

Letter Cards for Building, Blending, and Extending
1. Word Families

b	c	d	f	g	h
j	k	l	m	n	p
r	s	t	v	w	y
z	sh	fl	fr		
at	an	ad	ap	ag	ot
op	og	et	eg	en	un
ut	ug	ip	ig	ill	

Letter Cards for Building, Blending, and Extending
2. Digraphs and Blends

sh	h	s	ch	c	th
wh	t	st	sp	sk	sc
sm	sn	p	l	pl	sl
sw	bl	cr	fr	cl	fl
bl	br	gl	gr	pr	tr
dr	k	qu	tw		

at	ot	it	an	un
in	ad	ed	ab	ob
ag	eg	ig	og	ug
ill	ell	all	ick	ish
ack	uck	ash	ush	

Letter Cards for Building, Blending, and Extending
4. Short Vowels and Final Clusters

a	e	i	o	u	
b	c	d	f	g	h
j	k	l	m	n	p
r	s	t	v	w	x
y	z	sk	st	ft	lt
lk	sh	ch	th	ng	nt
nd	nk	mp		or	ar

Blank Template for Picture Sorts

Blank Template for Word Sorts
